SEARCHING FOR A BLACK WRITER

Maya Johnson

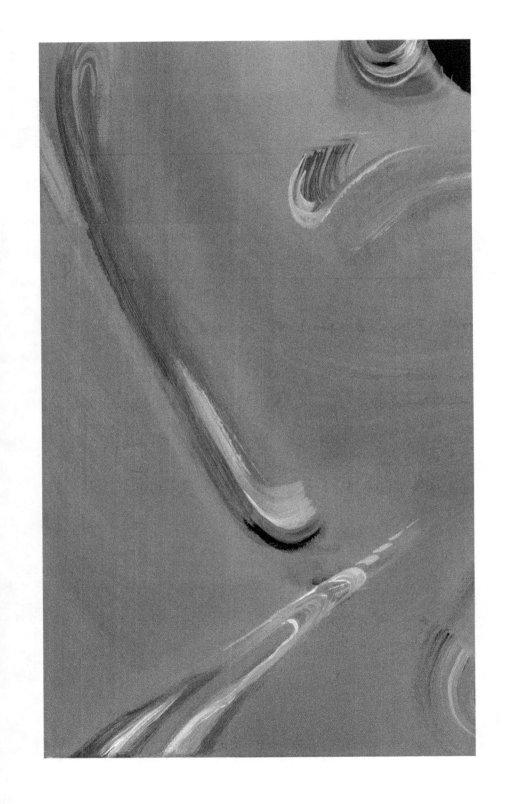

SEARCHING FOR A BLACK WRITER

Book design by Sonny Yiu
Illustrated by Giulia Zappia

The lines on page 128 are from "As", by Stevie Wonder, copyright by A Motown Records Release; © 1976 UMG Recordings, Inc.

The line on pages 168 are from "Home," performed by Diana Ross, produced by Quincy Jones, copyright by ©1978 Geffen Records

Searching For a Black Writer

Copyright © 2024 by Maya Johnson.

All rights reserved.

No part of this book may be used or reproduced without written consent of the copyright owner.

For privacy reasons, some names, locations, and dates may have been changed.

Printed in the USA
First Edition
ISBN: 979-8-8693-5943-8
Book cover by Sonny Yiu
Illustrations by Giulia Zappia

For my grandmother.

"I was alone in the world. It was not a small accomplishment. I thought I would die doing it. I was not happy, but that seemed too much to ask for."

-Jamaica Kincaid, Lucy

Contents

Preface 11

In Santa Barbara 17

Part I Self

Searching for a Black Writer 20

To Render 39

Mother of Longing 65

Part II Finding Home

Don't Want My Desire to Be the Color of You 85

Home 116

Death and Ancestors 131

Namesake 165

Acknowledgements 179

Preface

At the beginning of my senior year at UC Santa Barbara, I proposed this book as a research project to the Diana Raab Writing Fellow Program–a mentor-based fellowship that supported and funded me in the endeavor of writing *Searching For a Black Writer*. My proposal read as follows:

"*Searching For a Black Writer* will be a primarily nonfiction anthology exploring how trauma impacts our ability to accurately remember our experiences. This hybrid collection will be primarily nonfiction, but use the practices of fiction to fill in gaps between memories. This memoir-adjacent work will paint the landscape of my social and political identities through separately intense and minor traumas surrounding race, religion, class, and sexuality."

I defined this book first through therapeutic writing and fiction writing, and it was only later that I fully committed to the idea of a memoir. As a result, I've only now realized that nonfiction does not quite encapsulate what this project is.

This book is certainly not fiction either, but in my writing I have shaped my experiences into a narrative of emotional truth; *my* emotional truth.

I began with a collection of unpublished pieces–some fiction, some nonfiction–that I had written over my three years of university about my family and about my relationships. As someone who has always been a fiction writer, I found it difficult, confusing even, to be honest through nonfiction. Not only because it was so vulnerable, but because my memories were so hazy.

And, the more I wrote and delved into my past experiences, the more I realized just how much I had been hiding from myself.

It is natural for our bodies to hide painful memories from us. But it did not, and still does not, feel right to claim anything written in this book as the full truth. I don't believe myself in any way to be righteous, I am just the only one in the relationships I've written about who has taken the time to sit down and write about them.

When I was in my freshman year of college, I was tasked

in a writing course to read a chapter from Friedman and Silver's *Handbook of Health Psychology* called "Expressive Writing, Emotional Upheavals, and Health." James Pennebaker's expressive writing paradigm seeks to explain how or why only certain people who've experienced trauma end up with adverse mental and physical health effects. The initial studies done by the authors of that chapter produced evidence supporting the theory that writing about trauma, or of "major conflicts or stressors" in one's life, produces beneficial effects to mental and bodily health. Particularly they found the key to creating such change to be in "confronting the emotions and thoughts surrounding deeply personal issues."

The effectiveness of therapeutic writing, while scarce in the academic sense, has been abundant in my life. I've often written in diaries and journals, created fiction to work through an emotional event, or crafted letters when words did not come out easily. I believe writing comes instinctively to humans in stress.

Not long before I had taken that class, I'd gotten my heart broken. It was a familiar feeling as I fell in love so often; the same helplessly naive, all-consuming experience that I'd felt a million times over. I remember the morning that I knew it was over: I'd spent the night choking back tears at a party and pretending to be alright. I had no will left to cry. Leading with a primal instinct within me I knew—before eating, showering, or attending to any other needs–that I needed to write, and couldn't stop until *it* and *she* had all bled out of me.

I picked up an old piece that I'd been struggling with since my first month of moving to Isla Vista, and with a sudden ray of clarity I knew exactly where the story needed to go. As I wrote, the pattern of my past relationships unfolded before me like a map. I saw the choices I'd made over and over again reflected back through my words; different iterations of self reflected like a mirror. It was the same relationship over and over again.

Finally, as I wrote, I was able to cry.

Once, after a breakup, I wrote that I felt "I have this need to love wholly and deeply, to get my heart shattered like glass," because "deep down I love how poetic the pain is." Not my most original musing as a writer, in fact it makes me cringe to read it. But, the last line runs through my mind often these days, as I poke and prod at my own suffering with a spile trying to broach from it some beautiful work of art. It seems that's all we artists ever do.

I wanted to see if this messy process itself could be therapy; picking at the scab of old wounds, digging into the torn, bloody flesh to find some shrapnel of metal never originally recovered. If I removed it, could I fully heal?

This project was the result of years of emotional and mental repression; little issues that repeated and repeated and slowly ate away at my sense of self. It is why I feel the need to express, again, how subjective all of my written experiences are.

I wanted to write this book so that I could redefine myself and choose, carefully, where I would to move in the next phase of my life, instead of letting my trauma decide for me. I wrote it as a form of therapy. For so long, my psyche was a pot of stew left to simmer, bubbling over and splashing the kitchen.

As writers, we daily unearth our own darkness and put it on display, even if no one comes to look; even if we're the only one looking. That in and of itself is a beautifully transformative thing.

In Santa Barbara

I overlook the ocean. The waves sparkle white and yellow, blowing a restless wind over hot skin. We sit together, Santa Barbara and I, in a moment fleeting and yet infinite, looking forward, past our time together.

One day, I will pack all my things and leave this place behind. For now I will just be.

Part I
Self

Searching For a Black Writer

Carelessly scribbled onto a piece of loose-leaf paper, the note read:

I am in search of a Black writer for a project. If you are interested, please give me a call at this number. This is a landline—no text pls. Thanks :)

An older woman tapped me on the shoulder and slipped the note into my hand. I watched her crouched, spindly figure slip away between the rows of foldaway chairs; behind the balding man taking notes on a Santa Barbara Writers Conference pamphlet and in front of the legs of the hopeful blonde clutching a pink notebook to her thighs.

"What was that?" Sarah asked, leaning over my lap. Despite being in a room of fully grown adults, I felt like a teenager whispering in the back of a class, fearful the panel of speakers would snap their heads toward us and tell us to put our phones away. Sarah, Saraphina, and I—the three girls attending on a university grant—were the only people under thirty in the room. I was one of only two black people there.

I shook my head, unable to shake the cat-like paranoia of a woman being watched.

"I'll tell you later."

On the second floor of the Mar Monte Hotel, overlooking downtown Santa Barbara, a panel of published authors and agents introduced the conference. They went on and on about how much we were going to learn in the next few days of publishing panels and writing workshops. Through the window behind the panelists' heads, I watched crowds of boats bob on the ocean's surface.

The day before, a group of billionaires had made news when their submarine went missing somewhere above the wreck of the Titanic. At that point, everyone assumed that the ship had imploded. I imagined it somewhere outside the window, below the gray-blue waves on the Santa Barbara sea floor, sucking into itself like a vortex and taking everything with it.

My dad was the first person outside of the conference that I told about the note. When I phoned him a week later, he laughed. Then, he asked if I had called her back yet.

"Why would I do that?" I asked.

"Why wouldn't you?"

When I got the note, I felt shock, slight disgust, and the strangest sense of flattery. I laughed imagining someone writing this note in a fervor, pen pressed to thigh, ink staining her designer skirt at the sight of brown skin from the corner of her eye. She must have been so proud of her find; what a rare find.

But, to my dad, the goal of me going to school in Santa Barbara was to have opportunities like this. I was about to enter my third and final year in my university's writing program with little to show for it besides a few small publications and three years of work experience in fast-food restaurants. I was one year away from becoming a failed writer.

So, part of me really did want it to be real–that feeling like I'd been discovered, found. That I could be something special.

At five years old, I was an artist, an escapist. I scribbled in the gaps of my reality with stubby colored pencils, scattered paper, and Legos and Polly Pockets in the playroom of my family's old house in North Long Beach, the first place we ever actually owned, my parents and I.

It was where my mom taught me to read my first chapter book and where I wrote my first stories.

As years passed that glorious play space–the big room with

the sliding glass door where we sang to Far Far Away Idol and sipped apple juice from a plastic kitchen set—wore away. The creamy ceiling tiles browned and rotted and broke away at their corners, allowing in all kinds of buzzing wasps and spiders, and the door to the backyard would not close properly. I didn't think about that stuff until it became broken enough for us to leave; back then, it was just my castle.

I remember drawing myself. I was beautiful, all grown up and tall, dressed in a pretty red dress, a pair of pretty red shoes and a pretty red handbag. And I remember wanting to show my mom because Mommy liked it when I drew her things. I wanted her to be happy and proud, to scrunch her nose and tell me, "You did so good, lovie," as I presented it to her.

She looked at me in confusion. "What's this, lovie?"

"It's me!" I smiled so big.

I watched her excited smile fall and a now-familiar grimace replaced it. She began to yell:

"What is this? This isn't you. Do you look like this? Does your sister look like this? Your Daddy?"

Mommy didn't like that beautiful me had hay yellow hair down to her waist or that her skin was the same color I used to draw in the sand on the beach. Beautiful me was supposed to be brown; Brown like my family, and like my neighbors, and like my reflection.

But not like my mother. She is not blonde and White, but she is not quite Brown either.

I didn't know a beautiful brown version of me, but wanting to be something else was just shameful.

I was unhappy with my reflection for so many years after that: unhappy with my big round nose, puffy cheeks, and short frizzy hair. I always assumed that things would just get better as I got older: my hair would be different, and my nose would fit my face better, and I would be happier.

I wonder if I understood then that my skin wouldn't fade until I was just as light as the drawing. I don't know why I felt like we should all be so unhappy with who and where we were.

I never had any reason to want to leave my home in that neighborhood. My favorite home videos were in that house, eating mud from the front lawn, bathing in a chalk-filled kiddy pool. I loved the neighbors who had watched me grow up. But in 2008, my parents lost the house.

That neighborhood wasn't safe enough for us to grow up in anyway, my dad told me later.

They always wanted more; my parents did. They wanted my sister and I to have more opportunities growing up and they did. They wanted a nice house in the suburbs and for my sister and I to go to prestigious universities. To go further, somewhere foreign, somewhere we could brag about.

But how could I want them both, the house and its memories, and that beautiful rich, white version of me? The comfort and the absolute foreignness.

Back then, my Blackness was something of a harmony, a warmth surrounding me in what I knew, giving me a sense of self. As I left that house, it became stilt, thin and tall, lifted up from the surrounding land, fragile. But wasn't that what I wanted?

The opening night banquet of the Santa Barbara Writers Conference–the night I was passed the note—is one I remember through a drunk haze. I had never drank wine that expensive or strong before. A very kind woman I met at the bar felt endeared to me and offered to buy me a glass for 20 dollars.

I was standing in line, trying to discern the likelihood of getting carded (as I was only 20 years old at the time), when the woman introduced herself to me. She complimented my hair, the bright orange I'd dyed it after high school to distract from how much I disliked its appearance. My mother said that dying my hair so unnatural was something only white girls could do. I thought that if I was always going to be the only Black girl in a room, I might as well stick out for something other than my skin.

I think the other writers, always searching for their next

story, looked at me–my brown skin, bright orange hair, and hot pink lipstick–and wanted to collect me. I was something peculiar to them. And I was more than happy to let them–as long as I got something in return.

"I think you guys may be the youngest group here," the woman said gesturing, to my classmates across the room, her scarlet-red bob grazing my shoulder. She looked like someone who liked to stand out in a crowd, and put effort into doing so. I didn't like how close she was to me, but I smiled and laughed.

"Well, we're the only ones here on a grant from the University. It's a little intimidating, everyone here is so experienced."

"Don't let them scare you off. They all want what you have."

As I wondered what she meant by that, I eyed the man in the tweed suit approaching the bar in front of us. He didn't once look up from his conversation as he ordered a glass of wine and pressed a 20 dollar bill to the countertop. The bartender gave him no change.

"I'll try not to," I said.

I did the math in my head. A 20 dollar glass of wine, plus the 40 dollars or so I was spending on Ubers to and from the conference, plus the 700 dollars in attendance, which I was paying out of pocket until my grant check cleared. 760 dollars. My bank account would be drained. But I couldn't sit in this fancy hotel with all these seemingly fancy people and not have a glass of wine.

I was next in line. I hesitated and smiled at the woman.

"What kind of wine do you have?" I asked the bartender. He was tanned and beautiful.

"Just red or white," he said.

"Like Moscato?" I shrugged to the woman, and she laughed, approaching the bar next to me.

"We only have a Chardonnay. Try this," the beautiful bartender responded as he poured a splash into a clear plastic cup. It tasted nothing like the Chardonnay I'd had at my grandmother's last Christmas, which was bitter and vinegary. It was not sugary and peach-flavored like the five dollar wine my roommate and I liked to share either. It was perfectly in between.

"I'll take a glass of that," I said.

The beautiful bartender filled a beautifully angular wine glass right to the top and slid it towards me.

"I'll take the same," said the woman, pulling out her card.

"Oh, you don't have to," I blushed, unsure if I should be embarrassed or flattered.

"It's my treat."

I decided to be flattered as she swiped her shiny silver credit card and grabbed her glass by the stem.

"Don't let them get to you," she winked as she walked back to her table. "Remember, they're just jealous."

The drink and the comment went straight to my head. I desperately wanted to take the glass home–this beautiful, angular piece of glass–like it was a treasure. But I did not; I did not want to be *that* Black person. Not when I had woken up that morning fully determined to finally be a real writer and adult.

I knew there was a high likelihood I would be one out of three Black people in the room; I often was. I knew there was a likelihood I'd be one of the youngest people there. What that had made me a target of what I couldn't quite figure out. Was it amusement? Disdain? Envy?

At dinner, the other grant girls and I struggled to keep our heads above water with the adult writers. As we sat down for dinner, a group of them split us up and made pets of us, having each of us sit at a different one's side for amusement. To get to know us better.

"They offered him 20k for the first 20 words, and he just never did it! Can you imagine?"

No, I couldn't imagine, I told the woman sitting to my left as she laughed on a mouthful of steak and potatoes. I couldn't imagine ever turning down that much money–I didn't even know what that much money looked like.

"How old are you, again?" she cooed. I was 20 at the time.

"Just twenty? Oh, you're a baby. And what do you write, fiction? Oh, how cute. So, so cute."

A girl in her 20s never wants to be cute. She wants to be impressive. Hot. Professional. Taken seriously. Never cute.

Someone tapped me on my shoulder from behind.

"Hey! Uh, my memory's not too good, but did you say you had a spare lodging earlier?"

I turned around in my seat and met the blushed face of my fiction professor, Harvey Sullivan. He was the first faculty member I met at UC Santa Barbara, and one of the two Black professors in my writing program.

At first, he had reminded me of my grandfather, my mother's father. He had a kind of Blackness that was only recognizable to other Black people or someone who was from the South—as he himself described it. He had pale, nearly white skin and short, curly hair like ramen noodles. In every room he entered he inhabited some indescribable otherness I could only think to call Mariah Carey Black. He told me I reminded him of his daughter, a half-Black, half-Chinese girl. This was all we had in common.

For my first year of university, I was convinced that this man was the most well-connected person I would ever meet in the publishing industry and that he was destined to push me toward my goal of becoming a published author. My reasoning was that he had once been a New York Times bestseller (a title more impressive than the reality of his career) and of course, this meant I had to impress him.

With time, I found the truth. He wasn't good for much besides a few old stories retold, and retold, and retold.

Yet, it was through him that I got my first publishing opportunity, 150 dollars for a piece of flash fiction I wrote as a class exercise. It was a scathing evaluation of my family, a half-baked think-piece on Blackness and religion and my own shame. It was something I had never planned to publish; it felt more like a chunk of my soul than something anyone else needed to read, and it was not a chunk I liked. It was the part of me that was ashamed of where I came from. The naive, blameless version of me I was pretending to be.

"This is what you need to be writing," was what Harvey had told me.

At the conference, I looked back at the man, short, despite me being seated and him standing, glassy eyes and slightly red in the face.

"Did you say you had a spare lodging?" he repeated.

There was something unsettling about the way he said it as an awkward sort of joke–was he asking to sleep in my hotel room? Or was he just asking to sleep with me?

I laughed back, as I had all night, but told him I did not have a hotel room and that I lived near the school.

"Ah," was all he said as I waited for him to recognize me and ask how I was doing. He did not and instead he walked off with a nod.

The woman to my left strained her neck watching him go. "So, you know Harvey?"

"Yeah, he's one of my professors." I said, trying to shake the strange feeling he'd left me with.

"Oh, he's great! You're so lucky."

So everyone kept saying.

I set down my glass and looked around the room. It wasn't just him; all of the writers' faces had gone rosy, all laughing and chewing belligerently. Was everyone here plastered? The woman next to me was talking herself red in the face as she picked at her plate. Mine had already been picked clear, and I wondered if it was gauche to go back for seconds.

I hadn't eaten very much the last week, mostly living off stolen food from work: tater tots and chicken wings and bites of old pizza in between shifts. The night before, I'd stayed up until 1 am feeding loud, drunk college students and working my muscles to a tight ache. I was constantly broke those days as I wasted any money left over after paying my bills on expensive clothes and hair to support this ever-beautiful, perfect version of myself I decided I had to be to fit in in Santa Barbara. I had to be better than. I'd always had to be better.

Yet in that moment, it didn't matter how much better I tried to be. I wasn't going to be taken seriously; I wasn't even considered. I was a grant attendee, gifted a chance to walk among writing gods, except the gods were more akin to the Wizard of Oz; big, loud talk of a silly man behind a glittery sheet. And I was a thing of amusement, a pop of color. I should have felt a feature of the room as much as the decorative wallpaper or a gilded lamp.

I was lured with a grant check that would not clear for three more months into being a diversity rep in every room I walked into. To be a Black writer there was to be used. Fodder for someone else's self-enlightenment. A blaxploitation admission essay.

"Are you guys ready to go?" Sarah hissed across the table once our sitters had left us alone.

As we were splitting an Uber, I couldn't leave without them. Saraphina nodded enthusiastically.

"Give me one second," I said.

I picked up my empty plate and walked past the buffet to the bar. The beautiful bartender smiled at me, and I bit my cheek, slightly embarrassed. I had never left a restaurant without asking for a box to go. I could tell he hadn't been asked that in a while, and though he raised his eyebrows, he did not laugh at me.

"Follow me," he said before leading me into the kitchen. It felt strangely normal that I should have been in there at all. But that night, I wasn't a staff member; I was a guest.

Outside of the Mar Monte hotel, Sarah, Saraphina, and I stood in the cold ocean air by the hotel's double doors. The moon hung low in a swath of gray clouds as I contemplated if the woman who passed me the note earlier that day wanted to pay me, and for how much? How much would it take for me to say yes?

The Uber drove us out of downtown Santa Barbara, up the 101 South, back through Goleta, and finally into Isla Vista. My apartment was empty now, only because it was summer. I lived with five roommates, three of us in each bedroom, and the apartment was usually so crowded that it was hard to breathe. Stacks of Caitlin's furniture and belongings crowded the living room as she prepared to move out. Someone was always moving out or in it felt; things were always changing.

I fell backwards onto the edge of my bed; grateful my bedroom was empty for once; that the frat house below my window didn't party as often in the summertime; that it was truly silent. Already, I was anticipating the sweaty kitchen of the restaurant I worked at, stretching hours long into the night again as soon as I finished the conference and my time-off ran up.

I pushed myself onto my stomach, hanging over the edge of my bed, and reread the now-crumpled note in the slip of moonlight that came in through the window. I laughed to myself. It was funny, wasn't it? How desperate I was for success?

So many people in my family had sacrificed so much for the idea of their posterity. I couldn't waste getting to go to school here. I needed to be better, do something great.

I called the number.

"I'm working on a docuseries about Zora Thurston," said the faceless woman. "It's going to be on Netflix, so you'd have to sign an NDA before I can tell you much about it. You do know who that is, don't you?"

Her small voice was clipped, and quick.

"You mean Zora Neale Hurston?" I asked. With my phone pressed to my ear I closed the Google Document I was typing notes into and searched the name she'd written. The first result: Zora Neale Hurston.

"Yeah, Zora *Thurston*, really important Harlem Renaissance writer. Netflix says we need to have someone Black writing on the team to get it greenlit, which I think is kind of–well there's a big push to have a Black perspective on these kinds of things now. You know, I'm South African myself, but that doesn't exactly count for much," She huffed with annoyance after this, as if it should have made all the difference.

"So, they need someone Black on the team, and I had someone–my partner, a biracial woman–but she got sick with Covid."

It sounded unreal, that this woman wanted me to work on

her Netflix show simply because I was Black. *The woman is an absolute joke*, I thought. Did she, did any of *them*, hear just how ridiculous they sounded?

But she had connections, didn't she? Netflix was a big name to drop on a dime. Was this the type of person who I had to impress?

"What do you need me to do?"

"I need you to make a pitch deck. Do you know what that is?"

I didn't and I told her so.

"Well, research pitch decks and look into making one. They want to present what the show is about, give an idea for it so people will wanna make it, you know?"

"How will I do that if I don't know what the show is about?"

"Just research Zora Thurston," she huffed. "You know who that is, right? Very famous Black author. My research is on a time in her life that's not very well known, but I can't tell you about it unless you sign an NDA. Oh, and I'll need some writing samples."

I took down the information she wanted me to, and I did the research on Zora Neale Hurtson. I prepared a portfolio and emailed her back and forth for days arranging for it to be faxed to her office and printed. I called. I called again. I waited days and days for her to get back to me to discuss rates or what she thought of my writing. I never heard back.

If Black writers were rare in Santa Barbara—so rare that she slipped through a crowd to find me—I assumed I had to have done something wrong. Maybe my emails weren't professional enough, or my samples must not have been good enough. But there was no way of knowing, so I had to let it go. If that wasn't enough for me to make it, I didn't know what would be.

To Render

Studying at a school like UC Santa Barbara should have been paradise. It was frat boys skipping class to surf three steps from their dorms. It was day-long ragers and girls in bikinis on a Monday. In Isla Vista, my college years were meant to be reckless, inebriated, and untouchable.

In the day, lit up in that bright ocean glow I had come to associate with Santa Barbara, the party town of Isla Vista was beautiful. It was nothing but thin, happy students everywhere, biking to classes and lounging half-naked on lush patches of greenery. Jasmine bushes and eucalyptus trees swallowed the rows and rows of colorful houses and brightly-painted apartment complexes. There, we all found ourselves caught between adulthood and our own immaturity. IV was a fantasy world where we could play pretend with our mothers' clothes and our fathers' money.

"I've never lived anywhere as nice or expensive as this," my dad told me the day we toured my new home for the first time. My apartment in Isla Vista would've cost 3600 dollars a month if I had lived there alone. But, split between six girls, it cost my parents 600 dollars a month.

My father wanted to ensure I knew how privileged I was to have this college experience. All year, he mocked me in our phone calls when I referred to Isla Vista as IV and threw jokes about how bougie I was had been getting.

On El Greco, the street in IV that I lived on for my three years of university, the rainbow graffiti and assortment of pride flags decorating the neighbors to our right, the housing co-op, starkly contrasted the junkyard in front of us that was frat row. Four fraternity houses shared the block across the street from my apartment on El Greco, old couches and homemade die tables collecting in the sand-filled parking lots. My third year of college, after my roommates and I finally got rid of our ratty old sectional couch, we found it again on a platform in the backyard of Kappa Sigma two weeks later. It was the Island of Misfit Toys. The impermanence of a place like that was strange and often beautiful.

But, something changed in Isla Vista when the sun went down. Isla Vista was known for being a never-ending party. Whether it was a weekday or weekend, once the town went dark, a never-ending stream of girls in crop tops and mini skirts, and boys with open shirts dangling beer bottles flooded the streets. Music blasted from the frat houses and open apartment windows while groups of students laughed and shouted and stumbled about. It didn't take long for me to notice the uncertainty and insecurity always present in their flitting glances; the thing that the darkness seemed to draw out of us.

One of the first things that I learned about Santa Barbara once I had moved was that it is overwhelmingly white. This became my insecurity.

Somehow, I didn't know this fact before I arrived. All of the colleges that I had applied to had low percentages of Black students–this was expected in California–though none as low as this one. In Long Beach, where I grew up, I never felt like a minority. My classmates in school were a mix of everything–Black, Latine, Filipino, Cambodian. I thought UC Santa Barbara would be the same or similar. The school had a Black Student Union. I knew this because the girl who led my high school senior class in a tour of the campus–the cool neo-soul, Erykah Badu-listening girl wearing the patterned headwrap–was in it. That had to mean something.

I didn't realize then that Blackness in Santa Barbara would be something I would have to search out. If I stayed within my natural circles: my classes, my new roommates, and work, not only would

I often be the only Black person in the room, but I'd be in a culture where it often felt like my peers didn't fully understand me.

To top it all off, my self-imposed expectations of success quickly conflicted against the pressure of becoming a real college girl: someone who drinks and parties and makes out with strangers, having wild, abandoned fun–despite the fact that I had never done any of these things. I didn't think I needed to in high school. I studied; that was supposed to be enough.

Before college, I had a singular idea of who I was as a person; or at least who I should have been. The best version of me–the version I wanted to be–was intelligent, respectable, high-achieving, and focused.

In Santa Barbara, without the people and places that had defined me and my choices, I was suddenly free to become anything; I could lose myself in the drugs and the drinking and the fucking of it all so easily.

I chose to attend UC Santa Barbara because I knew this. I wanted to run from all I knew and create something new. Writing fiction there of all places should have been the perfect choice. So, why did it all feel hollow?

My love of writing started early in my childhood, instilled in me, largely, by my paternal grandmother. As a child, I always looked forward to trips to the bookstore with Grandma Ruby. My older sister, Margot, and I visited her often in my dad's hometown of Santa Monica, after service at the family's church on Sundays, or to spend the weekend at her apartment. Grandma Ruby would sit us down to watch an old film or obscure British television show she'd discovered while she cooked the most wonderful dinners—crispy salmon with boiled potatoes and sour cream, oven-baked fried chicken and green beans with bacon in them, skillet steak with mushrooms and caramelized onions. Each recipe was a mix of the Mississippi-grown southern comfort and health-nut Califonian attitude that I came to know her for.

My dad liked to say that Grandma wasn't just a Black person, she was "*the* Black person," the holder of all our family's ancestry and culture. She was tall and mysterious, and walked around her apartment with her head wrapped in a scarf like Sojourner Truth.

At night, my sister and I would sleep side-by-side in her bed while she slept on the couch in the other room, gently dozing off to *Pride and Prejudice* or *Meet Me in St. Louis*. I sometimes liked to sit at the kitchen table, watching her watch, stirring my bowl of mint chip ice cream until it turned to soup. To me, she was magical.

She was an optimist, my grandmother was; always committed to bettering herself and others. Each visit—because she knew how much we enjoyed it—Grandma Ruby would make time to take my

Margot and I to the big, two-story Barnes & Nobles in downtown Santa Monica. It was my favorite place to be, second only to her apartment.

While Margot and I scoured the young adult fiction, Grandma Ruby would wander the cookbook section, making note of recipes she wanted to try. After an hour or so, we would return with armfuls of books. Over the years, my shelves slowly filled to the brim with the books she bought me or lent from her own collection.

It was the fantasy of fiction that really drew me to writing; the escape from reality. Besides time spent attached at the hip to Margot, or time spent with my family, I spent a lot of my childhood and adolescence alone, stuck in my own imagination.

I was the type of kid that adults would marvel at, telling me how mature I was for my age and how quiet and well-behaved I was; a well-kept pet. This kind of praise let me know that I was doing things right; that I was one of the "good ones". If I hardly spoke, it was out of worry that the words that came out of my mouth would be "wrong" in some way.

In a Black household, I one day learned, discipline meant something different than it did for my non-Black classmates. My mother and father were teachers—one at an elementary level, the other high school. Rules and strict punishment came naturally.

For our Black household, discipline started with restrictions on what kind of things my sister and I could read and watch. No Cartoon Network past 7pm, no Teennick. Definitely no MTV, and a big, whopping, leave-the-theater no to *The Hunger Games*. As we matured, it was what we could wear, who we could hang out with and where. There was to be no television on weekdays, no makeup or scandalous clothes, no profanity, no boyfriends, and no sex.

It made sense to me that when I broke a rule as a child, the punishment was physical. As I got older though—too old to whoop—many of my punishments were self-inflicted. I quickly internalized my parents' judgments. If they did not punish me for a transgression—and I had many—my guilt would do it for me.

Grandma's house had no rules, though. She didn't care what I watched or read, just that I did. I didn't have to monitor myself.

In the journals she bought me, I began to write stories. I wrote when I should have been sleeping. I wrote during the school day. I wrote at night instead of doing my homework. I wrote on car rides and during sermons at church. I wrote until the covers were ripped and peeling and the pages worn bare with eraser marks.

I wrote so much that my third-grade teacher, Ms. Fittinger—once brought to exhaustion by my disregard of her class and the sight of my head, tucked into a book—confiscated my favorite journal as a punishment.

"You can get this back at the end of the day," said Ms.

Fittinger as she snatched the notebook from my desk and snapped it shut between her fingers. As my classmates oohed and aahed at my delinquency, she slipped it into a cupboard in the back of the classroom.

"If you bring it in again, Maya, I will get your parents involved. You need to be paying attention in class, not scribbling."

Before the day was out, I came up with a plan for my friend Isaac and I to get it back: the Big Heist. We snuck into her classroom during lunch, claiming that Isaac had left something inside of his desk, and replaced my sparkly red composition notebook with an empty black-and-white one. I was so nervous my whole body trembled, but I felt furiously vindicated; why should anyone get to take away what meant most to me?

Ms. Fittinger noticed the switch before lunch was out. She took away both notebooks, then called my mom to school to discuss how inappropriate it was for me to spend all my time reading and writing in class, even if I had finished my work. She emphasized how this kind of thing would not roll in middle school—a thing teachers liked to say when they wanted a kid to act more mature than they needed to be. It really meant:

"You won't be a kid forever. Grow up."

But it did roll in middle school, and in high school, and in college afterward. I started novels on loose pieces of scrap paper, and, if I wasn't writing, I was staring off into the distance, daydreaming up a story. In high school, I'd stay up until the early morning writing fiction in bed. I graduated with nearly 200 thousand words written and a stack of filled journals.

Despite Ms. Fittinger's warning, I went on to live most of my life half-present, half-occupied in a fantasy or daydream. By the time I reached fifth grade, it was my mom who started to notice signs of depression. It wasn't until my sophomore year of high school that I really felt something was wrong.

Each morning of sophomore year, I'd get off the bus and walk towards the school entrance, past groups of kids that hung out on the grass in front of the Lakewood High sign, and a hot, trembling feeling would come over me. I would feel their eyes on me, feel as much as I felt I had two feet and ten toes that they were all judging me; studying the minutiae of my hair or my outfit.

"What a weirdo," they'd all think about me.

"What's wrong with her hair?"

"Where do you think she gets her ugly clothes? Doesn't she know she's outgrown those jeans already?"

I was too tall, too lanky, too quiet, too frizzy.

This kind of internal dialogue followed me throughout each day; in every period of every class, constantly. It was exhausting. And so, to quiet it, I started waking up at 5:00 a.m. each day, two hours before my bus to school arrived. For those two hours, I'd try my best to make my hair lie flat, to make my eyebrows perfectly arched, and erase the creases under my eyes. I even cut the stomachs off my t-shirts and bundled myself up in an oversized jacket to sneak it all past my parents before going to school. I thought what I needed was a "glow-up". To be prettier, sexier, and more attractive. I thought that would fix things.

I still didn't have words for the way my mind ran nonstop, criticizing everything I did. I was never good at speaking words to my emotions; they always came out wrong. I only knew that I, or it– whatever *it* was–needed to be fixed.

When I wrote, though, I felt completely in control; like I could put everything wrong in the world into its proper place. It was the only thing that felt good, that got the thoughts out of my head.

Grandma Ruby also wanted to be a writer at some point. I believe she would have been one, too, if she hadn't had to drop out of school in the fifth grade. I knew it was the fifth grade exactly because she told me so when I interviewed her for my middle school family tree project. From then on, she told me, she worked with her parents and siblings on the farm they sharecropped in Mississippi, so she never finished her formal education. But, she still loved to read. Grandma Ruby had a great collection of books: cookbooks and mystery novels and old British literature; Jane Austen and Agatha

Christie scattered all around her apartment.

She is the reason I began to work towards being an author so early: because she wanted a writer in the family.

Throughout adolescence I began to picture myself leaving home to be a *real* writer like Rory Gilmore, head of the school newspaper at Yale, or Allen Ginsberg, frantically typing away in the dorm room at Columbia. They were incomplete dreams, based in fiction. But they were all I had to guide me.

In my first term at a real university, three months after transferring to University of California Santa Barbara, only one fiction class was offered within my writing program. To get into the College of Creative Studies, I submitted a meticulous portfolio of my short stories and high school essays in a desperate attempt to prove I could write. I was told that only a few people would make it through admission.

Unlike the rest of UC Santa Barbara's campus and all its beautiful, newly-built lecture halls overlooking the ocean, equipped with electronic whiteboards and swivel seats with charging ports, the College of Creative Studies was built sometime in the 1960s. It had since become a stretch of multi-use classrooms for the College's Writing, Art, Music, and Biology programs. Each class had its own piano, some had sets of easels propped in their corners and paint splattered across the walls. Compared to the rest of the campus, CCS felt accessible, and safe, if a bit rough around the edges.

My first-year fiction workshop was held in an old conference room. A long, low wooden table stretched the length of the room and a projection screen hung limply over the chalkboard in front of the class. The room smelled sweet, like dust and old books and chalk.

When I arrived each day, a stout, caramel-colored man named Harvey would be sitting at the end of the table, pushing clementine oranges and chocolate-covered cookies towards us. And *he* wanted us to call him Harvey. Almost all my professors in CCS wanted to be called by their first names. It was progressive and created less of a power dynamic between professors and students, they argued.

Harvey started each class like a substitute who hadn't expected to be given an extra class that day.

"Well, we're all here," he'd say, lifting the loose cloth mask off his lips. Lips that smacked as he paused, looking for the next words to say. He'd begin on some tangent:

"Who here has read Kate Chopin? What, no one? Wow. You guys should really know her; she's a very important uh... woman writer. Wow, what are they teaching you guys, anyway?"

With wide eyes, he'd chuckle dryly and cough over the edge of his mask.

"Colleges can't really teach anyone how to write, though.

You'll realize this if you ever get into the publishing world. Lots of educated people with money who can't write for shit in publishing. And some people with no experience who end up making a lot of money!"

From the way he said it, I understood that he was not one of these people.

"But the industry and agents are assholes, anyway. You know, actually, I should bring in my agent for you guys. That'd be a good experience for you all; to meet a *real* agent."

He gave off the air that he believed himself to be a misunderstood genius. I disliked his cockiness, but who was I to say that he was not?

In this fiction workshop, there was a random scattering of people across campus who thought they could write. I was one of them. The others: several senior STEM students in need of a creative arts elective, some pompous English majors, and a few undecided fantasy novel lovers. There was also another first-year from CCS, and our professor: a published author, who had once made it onto the New York Times Bestseller's List. At the time, though, I knew him to be exclusively published in online literary journals.

Before coming to UC Santa Barbara, I spent a year attending community college classes via Zoom to get a head start on my education while sequestered by the Pandemic. During that time, I learned that fiction writing was something many people felt they could easily do at some point in their lives: recent high school graduates like myself, 30-year-old stoners, retirees, and adult professionals with full-time jobs. In some people's eyes, all it took to be a fiction writer was to think up a story and put a few words to the page.

This theory was tested when my class had to workshop my 30-year-stoner classmate's short story. It featured him and a classic sitcom character smoking in a palace on the moon, surrounded by naked middle-aged women who would only wake to have sex with him or offer to make him pancakes. Bryan didn't understand what I meant when I asked him:

"Don't you think it's a bit *objectifying* to have the protagonist squeeze the unconscious woman's breast with his foot?"

It was hard not to feel that hinging all my hopes and dreams on fiction wasn't a mistake at this point. I wanted to believe that there was something important for me to learn from Harvey.

I did not want to end up a failed writer–not just a bad writer, but someone who never accomplished anything through it.

For the first few weeks of my time with Harvey, he wanted us to write vignettes. He opened class by reading us something he'd published recently in an online journal about an albino boy he knew while growing up in New Orleans. The boy was so white you "wouldn't know he was Black if your family wasn't Black."

The boy was a bit of a town freak, according to Harvey's writing, and burnt down his family's house. According to local gossip, he did so to make his room as black as he wanted to be. I didn't get the point of the story, but Harvey seemed to think it was very poignant. And I wanted to impress him by "getting it."

"Render," Harvey told us. "It takes so much effort to imagine and to create and most people aren't very good at it. Try to render instead."

Despite the fact that this was a fiction class, not creative nonfiction, Harvey asked us all to spend the next 25 minutes rendering something; some experience. I couldn't think of a single important thing that I wanted to write.

Well, there was one thing–but it wasn't an experience I was ready to face.

Up until that point, I had chosen to write only fiction because it distanced me from reality; it was a distraction from my own life.

At community college, my first short story was about a woman with a proclivity for stealing. I'd shoplifted in high school, even got caught once and forced to pay a fine. This woman was different. She didn't just steal makeup from the beauty store. She liked to steal from other people; coworkers, neighbors, friends. She'd snoop around other people's homes and dig through their belongings; their diaries, purses, and fridges. She stole from other people what her own life lacked.

I wanted to be imaginative, and Harvey wanted me to render. As I sat there and tried to think of something to write–something that didn't have to do *that thing*–all I really felt was how much of a disappointment I was.

So, in my anger at not having anything to write about in fiction workshop—no interesting experiences of my own—I wrote about my parents. I wrote that my father didn't have any friends of his own except for his six siblings and that those were the only people my parents really spent time with. That they drove down to Carson to that seedy old bowling alley and sang karaoke on the weekends, and that before Uncle Leroy got married to a nice lady, Lee, he had a wild girlfriend I named Miss Lorraine, who wore glittery blue lipstick and stumbled drunk into my aunt's house on the Fourth of July.

I wrote that my family didn't do that type of thing. That my Uncle Ramon is the pastor at the church he and his siblings were all raised in, and that my cousins and I, at least from my perspective, were supposed to be good and churchgoing and proper. Well, I wasn't. And neither was Miss Lorraine.

I spit it all out onto the page and sat back, nearly heaving. I looked up to see Harvey eyeing me in a curious way. I could tell he wanted me to read, so my hand shot up when it was time to do so.

My voice was stuttering, as always when I read, but I tried to make it sound strong and important:

"No, my family doesn't do that kind of thing. We're the kind of family that chased off my cousin Elijah's girlfriend for being a bit too affectionate in my aunt's pool. The kind of family that masquerades partners as "friends" because my kind, and my Uncle Darren's kind, are condemned to hell.

No, in our family, God's Will comes first, and our wants and needs—each other's true selves—that comes second."

Even as I read it, I was sure my words couldn't capture the whole story. I was angry, resentful, and had written all the bad, but none of the good. None of the sunday dinners at Grandma Ruby's, none of my mother's warm smile with the scrunch in her nose, or my dad's almost annoying optimism, inherited from his mother. It felt incomplete, lacking perspective. I felt like I was airing out my family's dirty laundry. But Harvey said it was good.

"Very good," he said with a dry laugh. "You should submit that somewhere."

I tried not to smile; it felt cocky to accept a compliment openly. I also struggled to believe him. I always wanted to believe that

I was a good writer, but in truth, I needed a lot of validation to truly believe it.

As my classmates packed their bags and began to filter out at the end of class, I found Harvey watching me again.

"What are you mixed with?" he asked as if it was the most normal thing in the world.

I was standing behind my seat, sliding my laptop into its case when he asked me. It was something I got asked often in middle school, but not much since. It felt strange to be asked by a professor.

"Chinese, or some kind of Asian, I think?" I told him. "I've never actually taken an ancestry test, but my dad says that's what my mom's side is mixed with."

"Y'know, my daughter is half-Chinese," he said, pulling up a photo on his phone of a small girl whose skin was lighter than his. The girl in the picture had loose, curly hair and thin brown eyes. She looked nothing like me.

"You remind me of her."

I decided to take this as a compliment.

"Are you in the College of Creative Studies?" he asked.

I told him I was.

"You know, it's nice to see another Black person in CCS," Harvey chuckled, his mouth hanging half-open. "There used to be a bunch of us, but not anymore. Things have changed, I guess."

I struggled to imagine a version of Santa Barbara where Black people weren't one out of 20, but I liked the way he said it: another Black person, not just a Black student. It was like we were in it together.

As Harvey went on another tangent—telling me again how not all Black people look Black even if their families were Black and only other Black people could tell—I decided he reminded me of my Grandad. Their skin tone was almost the same, with the same round face and shiny bald spot at the top of their head.

"Have you ever been published before?" Harvey asked me.

"No," I told him, but it was a big goal of mine. At that point, my only goal was to be published by the time I finished college. Then, I'd be good enough. Then, I'd be a real writer.

"You're from the LA area, right? I have a writer friend who has this journal based there. I'll send you her information. You should submit. She does this festival for writers in May. I'll be there, and sometimes some students from CCS come. You should go. They'll find you very impressive."

I took this as meaning that *he* found me very impressive, and gleamed. I hadn't read anything he'd written besides the one story, but he made himself seem impressive, that he had an agent and was getting published left and right.

When I submitted *Miss Lorraine* to the publication, it was

accepted almost immediately. I didn't realize it then, but this was because Harvey had connected me directly with the editor. He was also a journal's founder and was published in most issues. There was no physical magazine, but there was a stipend of 150 dollars, which felt especially good. I was going to be published right beside my professor.

Our next class continued with a similar routine. After Harvey's opening monologue, he set aside 25 minutes for the class to "render", the products of which we would discuss for the rest of the class.

As I began to render for the second time, I suddenly felt I had a lot to write about, empowered by my writing capabilities. Specifically, I was thinking about my hair, which often became the topic of conversation in Santa Barbara. Harvey's class was the only time that quarter that I wasn't the only Black person in the room.

"What is that little hat you wear?" my roommates would sometimes ask about my bonnet. I'd get people asking to touch my hair, white girls asking me to recreate styles on them; all kinds of little inquiries that opened up my well of insecurities.

"Did you cut your hair? It was so much longer when you had the—what do you call them—dreads?"

Before I left for school, I had thought very carefully about how I wanted my hair to look, and what version of myself I wanted to become through it: feminine, desirable, accepted. For 25 minutes in fiction workshop, I wrote about that feeling.

When it was time to read, like before, I felt a burning in my stomach, but my hand shot up immediately.

I cleared my throat and practiced my voice again: strong, confident.

"As Black women, our hair forms a hierarchy. From when we're just little girls–getting our virgin locks pulled tight into afro puffs and braids with brightly-colored, plastic barrettes–we get a place on it. Long hair is most beautiful and to be desired. Short hair is not unless you're a strong, businesswoman-type, a radical sistah, or the wrong type of dyke. Those we try to avoid.

There are the Ebonys of the world, dark little girls whose hair would come up in thick tufts around worn braids. We made fun of those girls when a loose braid of Kanekalon hair was found on the playground, the style loosening, begging to be redone. Then, there are the Marlees of the world, the mixed girls whose genes got just the right amount of Black. Her hair is never nappy, no, she has long, flowy curls that could land her a Netflix original, the kind that falls down her back like the white girl hair we all refused to admit we envied."

I had been told before that in writing classes, there comes a point when your story stops being something you have to create and takes on a life of its own. Mine began in that classroom. From that day forward, the story was all I thought about, my real experiences in Isla Vista tapering off into fictional daydreams. For months, I lived the life of a fictional character, exploring insecurities I'd long hid.

And, like before, Harvey seemed to find my work important and profound. I dived into this feeling.

At the end of the three months of my fall semester, "Good Hair" became my second story to be accepted for publication, my first one over two pages. When I got an acceptance email from a small literary magazine, I screamed with joy and fell to the floor. I thought, I can do this; I have something to say.

Next semester, after the fiction workshop had ended, I checked the course list to see what classes my first-year cohorts and I had to take for the winter semester—"Literary Theory," taught by H. Sullivan.

"What is lit theory?" one of my classmates texted in the group chat made for our class as freshmen. Though I was technically a second-year transfer, I took all my classes with this group of twenty-something writers, and for several years, we grew alongside one another. We were an eclectic group, like most groups of writers are; all oddballs in their own ways.

"Does anyone know the professor?" Kit–the boy who

introduced himself at orientation as an ex-conservative—texted.

I was excited to say that I was the only one who had taken a class with Harvey, which made me feel ahead of the rest. I told them that he was eccentric and a bit strange, but nice, and that he was an author who had helped me get published the previous quarter. I didn't mention how I suspected he only paid me such special attention because I was the only Black student. It didn't seem as relevant.

"Is he a good writer? I think that his book is on the reading list," one of my classmates texted back.

I logged onto Gauchospace, and there it was: *Oh, The Mischief You'll Find* by Harvey Sullivan, listed on the class syllabus.

Vain, I thought, for a professor to put their own book on a reading list. But all the same, I was curious, almost excited to read it. It took about a week into the winter quarter for my book to arrive and for the group chat to start buzzing again. Thirty minutes before one of our Zoom classes with Harvey began, someone sent a photo into the chat. It was a page of the book.

"Uh, guys, has anyone read Harvey's book yet? Isn't this kind of weird?"

The next day, when my book arrived, I poured it over immediately. *Oh, The Mischief You'll Find* was the story of Harry Stewart, a 29-year-old Black professor at UC Santa Barbara who was troubled by his love life involving several undergraduate girls, including Tracie "the alluring twenty-one-year-old virgin," and Deja, "the foreign, forbidden student from the college he teaches, and holder of magical mysteries." In the first few pages of the book, Harvey's self-insert protagonist engaged in descriptive and vaguely consensual sex acts with Tracie while she lay asleep. That was the page my classmate sent in the group chat.

Within the next few days, all my classmates had read the book and came to the same conclusion: there was something deeply unsettling about Harvey. I felt disappointed in the quality of writing and its subject matter. Was this the man I had revered for a period of time?

Suddenly, each interaction I'd had with him was cast in a new light. I thought of how he'd described the girls and wondered how he would describe me:

The sexually-repressed Christian girl with mysterious oriental ancestry.

With this new thought, I reexamined what I had written in that class. I was conflicted because the only writing I had published was that which plundered my own privacy and pain for validation—for my male professor's validation, for some white editor's.

But, at the same time, I *was* proud of my writing. I was proud of what I had accomplished, and that I had gained confidence in myself as a writer.

Harvey told me that he had had people in his life cut him off for the things he'd written about them. He told me that was just part of being a writer; a risk we had to take. I wondered if my family would ever do the same.

I didn't know how to reconcile the feelings. I did not want to move forward as a nonfiction writer if it meant exploiting the people around me.

If that was what being an author looked like, I wasn't sure I wanted it anymore. And if I wasn't sure that was what I wanted, I didn't know what I was still doing there.

Mother of Longing

As the summer sun began to set somewhere between Placentia and Anaheim, my mother and I drove away from my grandma's apartment in silence. When I was much younger, my mother, sister, and I would visit my maternal grandmother every weekend. Lately, my mother and I were lucky if I was home long enough once in a season, and I had ruined that short time spent together by starting an argument. I felt justified in our fight, but I was just waiting for my mother to break that composed feeling.

It was one of our usual fights. They were always the same, whether I was 21, or 16. I always thought I was somehow old enough to be on equal footing with my mother. I think a daughter always wants to be understood by her mother.

It didn't matter why we were fighting; it never did, whether we were fighting about my hair or the outfit I hid under a sweatshirt to school that morning. A sink full of dirty dishes or the secrets she'd found hidden on my phone, like where I'd been the night before.

As we turned the corner onto the freeway, we exchanged low murmurs and quick back and forths.

"You know better than to do that in front of your grandmother."

"I didn't say anything wrong," I said.

"Watch your tone," she said.

Then, silence again. Burning. A gnawing. I watched the skyscraping body of Knott's Berry Farm pass on the left side of the highway. Supreme Scream rode up fast and dropped—the orange of the sunset smeared beneath the windshield.

Mommy started up again. This time was a bit louder, a bit harsher, but I remained tight-lipped, uttering little response though it was pulsing under my chest. At this point, my face burned, and we were moving so fast that I just wanted it all to stop. I felt dizzy. I was starting to doubt myself, doubt my feelings, doubt my mother.

Back home, the yellow walls of my bedroom, cast in the light of half-burnt bulbs, closed in on me. I heard her footsteps near the door and knew it was going to start up again. This was the part where she acted nicely towards me. She'd rev up slowly and tell me she loved me, pulling me sobbing into her chest.

It would still end in screaming. What was the point? She wouldn't stop until she'd won, and I couldn't think, I couldn't feel, I couldn't understand anything.

I screamed. "Stop. Please just stop."

My body balled over on the bed, sobbing, rocking, heaving. She looked at me, oscillating between the two versions of her I knew: compassionate, caring, loving. Disdainful. Then she shut the door. That time, she left.

It was not the first rift we had in our relationship, and it would not be the last. We were both fiery and determined, but saw the world in dramatically different ways, always ending up offending or hurting the other. It was the same for my mother and her mother. It was politics, sexuality, and the way I chose to live my life. I felt so deeply that if she just saw things from my perspective, she would understand. I desperately wanted to make her understand.

After our fight, I didn't know what to say to her. I knew that if I spoke, I'd only say it all wrong. So, I wrote it instead.

As a child, I wrote out everything I couldn't communicate with words.

I tore a page from my journal and slipped it under her bedroom door that night. When I was 10, it was pressed into an envelope. When I was 12, it was scribbled on my bedroom desk.

"I have had to fight and fight and fight just to exist as me. I will not downplay who I am to make you or anyone else more comfortable. I don't need you to validate my life and experiences. All I ever wanted was for you to accept me as I am. Flaws and all."

For my three years of university, I existed in a state suspended between my many homes. They felt endless. I'd spend a month at school in Santa Barbara, then a week at my parents house in Long Beach, and a weekend with my grandmother in Santa Monica. Then, a few days in San Jose before another trip back down; seven long hours being jostled down the coast in an Amtrak train to spend a month on the Isla Vista shore.

I didn't know when I left home that, from then on, I would spend every holiday, every birthday, and every school break trudging up and down the hallway of Los Angeles Union Station, weighed down by the weight of my belongings. The station building itself was a work of art: ornate stone floor tiles and glittering chandeliers hanging from beamed ceilings. When I first saw the station, I thought it was glorious. With time and familiarity, it became less so, its tall corridors smelling of piss and unwashed bodies, everyone hustling in sweat to their next destination. Long train rides were spent smelling lunch on the other passengers' breath, sleeping with my head knocking against the window.

 The day my parents dropped me off at university, they did so briefly. We loaded my college apartment—the 600-dollar spot I'd found on Facebook only a month earlier—with all the belongings I deemed necessary to start my new life: an unbuilt desk, my new office chair, produce boxes of books and plants and shoes, and two giant trash bags full of clothes. My roommate's old mattress was waiting for me on the top bunk, and the other girls' belongings carved out a corner of the room.

 When my mom told me that she, my dad, and my sister were leaving for home, I was sitting in what would soon become my corner of the bedroom in a scatter of nails, slats, and wooden boards. It was only 3 p.m. I had no car, only half of my last paycheck, and an empty fridge. But it was time for them to go—though, at the time, I did not understand how beating the traffic back through L.A. was a good enough reason.

 I hugged my mom, took a smooch on the forehead from my dad, and tried to remember how my sister acted when it was her turn to finally be alone. How did she feel? Was she scared? Relieved? Elated?

 I was surprised my goodbye didn't last longer. Surprised that my family didn't stay for burritos at Freebirds or to take a tour of the streets my dad still remembered. He had his own memories of this place, of IV Halloween and spending Deltopia in his best friend's apartment. It was my turn to make mine.

I had been preparing my whole life for the moment my parents would drive off from whatever place I had decided to be an adult in; the moment I would be alone. After finishing high school, the last place I wanted to be was in my parent's house. All I could think of there were the therapy sessions, the secret texts and phone calls, the screaming; the silence that filled the halls of that empty house suffocating me. Through the Pandemic I hungered for it, visualizing this scene again and again in daydreams and wondering what I would do with such absolute freedom.

I thought then, that I could just leave everything else behind.

But, in this moment of so-called independence, I still felt incomplete. I was missing the tools I needed to finish my desk—or vanity, really. It was a thin console with a huge mirror, and I had no hammer to drive in its nails. So, I hammered the thing together with the end of my new Hydro Flask and dented its back. The vanity was far too small for me to use as a real desk, but I'd already made my decision. I had to live with it.

For lunch, I ate chocolate chip muffins that my kind, new roommate had made and left on the counter, and later, the In-N-Out Burger she picked up for us. I was grateful for her support, and so did not dwell on how in incompetent it made me feel. Or how I wished my mother had been there to provide that kind of support instead.

I sat and sat and sat in that corner, the only place in the world that was now mine, and I wondered if I yet felt less or more lonely in that apartment than I felt in any of my parents and I's homes. When I ever would.

During the summer of my junior year of high school, getting driven to therapy by my parents were some of the loneliest moments I ever experienced. I knew on some level that therapy was what I needed—I'd felt since middle school something was wrong inside, like a big chasm in my chest—it just didn't happen how I wanted it to.

I started going to therapy once every two weeks after my parents had caught me with a girl.

In a tall, cubed structure in Eastside Long Beach, my mother and I were checked into our medical provider's mental wellness offices by a security guard in a tight metal booth. Upstairs, we sat in silence on a couch in front of a receptionist's desk as tension built between us. At half past, a tall white woman with a European accent and an obnoxious wart on the side of her nose led us into her office. It was covered in crayon art and colorful photographs, and the sun shone brightly through the window.

There was one of those typical blue couches off to the side—the kind you tend to see in movies. I could see a protagonist lying with their hands over their chest, divulging the truth of their childhood to some sympathetic old white man in glasses. Since my mother was there with me that first day, she got the couch, and I sat on a chair off to the side. The therapist sat at her desk and smiled at us with her dead eyes.

"Why don't you start by telling me why you're here today."

I knew why I was there, but it was hard to describe. I could only imagine myself in the shower, wet and shaking, with my phone balancing on the bath's ledge.

My mother turned to me. "Do you want to tell her?"

I thought of my heart beating as my mother asked me to unlock the phone. My slippery fingers failing again and again, being naked and wet and embarrassed in front of the piercing eyes of my mother.

I shook my head. I did not want to recount this all to a woman I did not know. I let myself become engrossed in my hangnails as my mother described my relationship with "that girl."

I pulled and picked at the hangnail until it bled. I did not want to think about sitting on the stool in my mother's bedroom as she and my father read back everything we'd done and said. They asked if I'd really allowed someone to do that, to say that, if I'd sent those pictures.

When my mother was angry, she spoke through gritted teeth

like an animal baring its fangs, the words slipping out in a clipped hiss. "When you're dressed, come *right here.*"

In my parents' house, I learned to hide a lot; to explore in secret, and to delete browsing history and texts. Those messages were the one piece of evidence that I never deleted over all those years. They were my relationship. They were my first love.

At the end of it all, they texted her, "These are Maya's parents. If you message or speak to her again, we will go to the police."

I never found out what happened to Amalee or spoke to her again. I never sent her the letter I promised I would. When I tried to reach out years later, I heard nothing back.

For years after, I would try to forget the sound of my mother's and father's voices during the spring of junior year. They bounced off the house's beige walls, bathed in nauseatingly artificial yellow light.

"Did you really tell her to do that? Let her do those things to your body?"

Tall, stretched-out walls, plaster crusted into the nooks and crannies.

"Did you really say *I like it when you call me a—*"

The therapist's office had the same walls. Dinghy white paint. Absorbent. I could just let them take it all in for me.

"I don't even know who you are, Maya. Is this who you are?" I heard my mom cry. I did not respond or turn to face her.

Instead, I developed a habit of picking at my lips or nails. When that wasn't enough, I scratched and pressed my nails into my skin. I wanted a physical pain to distract from what I felt inside. I needed it to be piercing.

On the day of that first therapy session, I found a broken razor at the bottom of my jewelry box. That was the first time I cut myself.

After that day, I met with the strange woman biweekly after school. This went on for months. I sat on the typical blue couch with my hands inside my sweatshirt, my hair undone, and my under eyes dark and creased. I did whatever Elena, my therapist, wanted me to. Whatever she thought would move me through my emotions. I painted streetlights in swaths of blue or an orange sunset meant to represent my future, and I mentally urged the clock ticking on her coffee table to speed up.

My mom was usually the one to take me to my sessions; she believed in it the most. On our drives to and from, she'd play the radio and only speak to try to check in on my progress subtly; to see if the therapist had successfully changed me in some way. She tried her best, I think, to understand me and what I had done. When my father did have to drive, the car was deadly silent. For most of that summer, he successfully avoided saying more than a word to me.

Outside of Elena's office, I spent most of my time alone. Over the summer, I saw no friends, was not allowed to leave the house on my own, and rarely left my room. My parents had already pulled me out of my extracurriculars as a punishment: no more Marching Band or Orchestra trips. And I had no access to a smartphone or a computer, no "access to the outside world," was how my parents put it to me.

I was left to reread old books like I had as a child, searching for relief and disconnect from fictional worlds. I spent a lot of time wondering when the therapy would start to make my family feel right again.

One therapy session, Elena suggested we sew a pillow filled with cherry pits, a sort of fidget toy meant to help with stress. We sat knees nearly touching at the edge of the blue couch, both our hands on the sachet as I sewed the last bit of the lining together. I hated that her body was so close to mine. I hated the smell of her: freesias and Listerine. My body rejected her like a bad organ transplant, or an infected piercing. She made me feel sick.

Days later, the little pillow began to stink, too, like our kitchen sink when the dishes had not been done, or like leftovers that were forgotten in the back of the fridge and rotted.

Most days, though, Elena and I just sat in silence. I played with my sleeves and my nails and my hair as she tried to find new questions to ask me, some way to convince me to speak.

"Where do you want to go to college?" she asked one day.

"I don't know," I told her, hugging my knees to my chest. Instead of looking at Elena, I was looking behind her, searching for a new spot on her yellow walls to fixate on. I knew it didn't matter where I was going to college anymore. Nothing I could do could fix how I'd broken my family.

"Okay. Well, what do you want to do for work when you get older?"

"I don't know," I told her.

"What are you good at?"

"I don't know," I told her.

When Elena wanted a better response she stopped talking entirely. She'd simply stare at me head-on and let the room fill with silence while she waited for me to break.

I clenched and released my jaw, twisting it from side to side as I decided if I wanted to speak. "I'm okay at drawing," I then said quietly, my eyes darting down. "I think I'm good at writing."

Elena scribbled something in the notebook balancing on her lap. "Okay, that's good. What do you write?"

In highschool, I wrote fiction, but I hadn't written much of anything at the time besides a few school essays. I didn't have the motivation to write, not even a diary entry—except for one thing.

"I wrote..." the sentence trailed from my lips, wispy as vapor.

I struggled to get my lips to agree with the words. They still didn't trust this woman and didn't want to tell her anything. I pulled my knees back up to my chest and forced the words out.

"I wrote a letter. To her."

"To your girlfriend?" Elena leaned in. "What did it say?"

I once fell in love with a girl who wanted to be in the Marines.

"It was just some things I never got to say to her, I guess," I told Elena, shutting down again.

When Elena tapped her pen on the desk as she did then, I knew that she was waiting for me to say more, expand on the tiny nugget of information I'd thrown her way, but I couldn't give her any more than that. I wasn't trying to be rude, I just couldn't say it.

"Does writing help you work through your feelings?" she asked.

I shrugged. "I guess."

The little blue clock on the coffee table clicked and clocked away.

"Okay, fine," Elena huffed. "I have an assignment for you, then."

Elena pulled down her glasses and shut her little notebook as she spoke to me.

"I want you to write out everything you want to say to your

parents."

I was confused. "Everything I want to say?"

"To your mother."

I didn't have anything I wanted to say. If anything, I wanted to stop talking altogether.

I kicked my legs down and sat up in my seat, leaning towards Elena. "She isn't going to like what I have to say or think. That's the whole problem."

Elena put down her notebook and folded her hands across her lap. She meant business.

"Maya, do you want your parents to trust you again? Enough to let you have your phone back? To see your friends?"

I shrugged. It didn't seem possible for things to return to how they'd been before. When my parents and I had fought before, time always seemed to turn things back to a sense of normalcy and forgiveness. I'd given up on that returning after my latest transgression. I'd gone too far, wanted too much.

"Just tell her that you're sorry," Elena said. "Tell her you know what you did was wrong."

"But I don't feel that way." My tone was petulant, insisting.

"Just try," Elena told me. "Write it."

When our session ended I waited in the lobby on the

building's ground floor for my father to arrive and drive me home. Usually he was sitting in his car, just outside the front door, waiting for me. In the uncomfortably tall lobby, there were two stiff leather couches pressed against a glass wall where I sat and watched the street while a stone mermaid spit up water. The parking lot was empty.

I had only my backpack from school with me. In it was a copy of *The Catcher in the Rye*, a college-ruled notebook, a pencil bag, and my middle school flip phone that was now to be used only for emergencies by my parent's discretion. I pulled out the phone and typed a message to my father,

I finished my session, where are you?

He did not respond.

I had been waiting for about 30 minutes when I saw Elena leaving the building for the day. Her sharp, heeled step stuttered as she exited the elevator at the other end of the lobby and saw me seated there. Her eyes fluttered open wide, but she did not speak. Elena pulled a thin smile that did not reach her eyes and kept click-clacking across the clean white marble towards her car.

When my dad arrived, he said nothing to me about his lateness, just waited for me to buckle my seatbelt and drove off.

Instead of taking me directly home, though, he stopped in the parking lot of a Marshalls. I wanted to ask where we were going, or why we had stopped there, but it felt wrong to break the silence. So, I sat quietly and obediently. My dad got out and went inside the store.

I dropped my head into my hands and began to cry. I didn't know how to stop, the ability felt beyond me. I had never felt so ignored, so disregarded by someone I loved so much.

I pulled out the notebook and began to write.

It was Elena who instructed me to write my parents' a lists of my regrets; to put down my pride and move forward. It was Elena who had me focus on school and make up my mind about college. College was something my parents could be proud of me for, it seemed the only redeeming thing about me in their eyes at the time. As a writer I could make awful things useful again.

I decided to apply to whatever was the easiest. The UC application let me apply to four different schools with the four same essays, so it was the only one I filled out. I let whichever school accepted me have me. Then, one day, my parents dropped me off in Santa Barbara with a chair and desk and ran off before afternoon traffic.

I thought that physically leaving home would solve all my problems, but I still wasn't happy in Santa Barbara. I struggled to remember ever being truly happy, except for when I was in love. Truthfully, I think I was very depressed, but I had no real reason or outlet for that feeling, so instead of facing it, I decided to forget myself in favor of loving someone else. I rewrote my reality once; I could do it again.

I fell deeply in love again during my sophomore year of college. I didn't dare tell my parents about this girlfriend until the two of us were speeding up the 101 freeway, half an hour into our six-hour drive to San Jose, going 80 miles an hour in the same car that my girlfriend would later crash on our one-year anniversary. I called my mom to let her know:

"I'm going up north with my girlfriend. We've been dating for about three months, and I'm going to stay at her house for a few days to go to Pride with her dads and her sister."

I don't remember exactly how my mom's voice sounded. Thin, maybe even a bit empty, as if she'd been expecting this or was holding it all in. I knew it was my choice, and it was a choice I had to make, but I still felt like I would break.

Part II
Finding Home

Don't Want My Desire to Be the Color of You

After my confession, my mother and I had little left to say to each other.

I hung up the call and gazed out the window at an empty highway, fenced in on either side by green grass and orange rock, as my girlfriend and I drove further and further from the city. The afternoon sun was just starting to beat down. Eli and I had six hours of road ahead of us.

My girlfriend's hand squeezed my thigh, and I met her eyes. She had a tentative, trying smile. I tucked a strand of hair behind her ear. Its inky darkness was stark against her cheek.

Eli didn't understand what was going on between my parents and I. If anything, my family problems were an awkward obstacle to her, something to forget as she turned the speakers up again and revved the engine of her beat-up BMW to race the Tesla beside us.

My stomach tightened as Eli pressed her heel into the gas pedal, an impish grin grazing her lips, but I said nothing to stop her.

My mother had a saying: "What happens in the house, stays in the house." It meant that I was not supposed to share family business with those around me, even if it had impacted me deeply. Though I did not fully believe in the saying, it was something I had internalized over time, and so Eli knew very little about my last relationship.

In turn, that meant that my parents didn't know anything about what was going on between the two of us.

That summer after we'd met—the first time that I agreed to go home with her—I learned that my new girlfriend was a speeder. That was just who Eli was, as a driver and a person. She was reckless, impulsive, and emotionally volatile. Though we had only just met in March of my first year at UCSB, we were already exchanging *I love yous* in June and speeding 80-90 miles an hour up the California coast. In a few hours, I would meet her parents, and we would all attend San Francisco Pride together.

Who Eli was as a person should have been clear to me from the first moment I met her, when she tried to sell me drugs. For 40 dollars a pop, she offered me a ziploc sandwich bag full of psilocybin mushrooms. Immediately, when she walked through the front door of my apartment sometime during fall semester without so much as saying 'hello' to me—as if every space she walked into belonged to her—I disliked her. I sat on my couch and stuffed my nose into a book, ignoring her presence as all of my roommates greeted her excitedly.

My bunkmate, Katy, had been anxiously awaiting a visit from her best friend for months. They were all old friends, my roommates and Eli, and because of that I was meant to instantly trust and like her.

Sitting down on the other end of the couch, Eli spread her legs like a boy and bent between them to dig into a big, gray backpack. She had long, wavy black hair that fell over her face as she did so, and wore only sweats and thin tank tops. Still, she did not say hello or ask my name, though I was sure it was because she already knew. From her bag, Eli pulled out a plastic ziploc with some gray, chunky material inside.

"Did you want to buy any?" she asked me.

The plan for the weekend was for all of my roommates to do shrooms together, and for me to join. Before Eli, I had agreed. Now, with her sitting before me, I turned up my nose.

"No," I said, lips pulled into a tight, dismissive grin. "I'm good."

"Oh—okay." Eli looked surprised by my rudeness, clearly confused as to what she'd done wrong, but curious as she leaned in closer. Her big brown eyes scanned my face, like she was looking for a soft spot to push through in my hard exterior.

I was wearing a pair of ratty pajamas, hair gathered up into a frizzy ponytail, expecting to be seen by no one. Her eyes felt heavy on me.

"Well, uh, Katy and I are going to go out for smoothies in a bit. Do you want to come?"

Eli dangled a purple vape pen in her fingers. The entire time I knew Eli, that thing was always attached to her.

"No, I'm fine," I said curtly, curling my legs up towards me. I did not know why she was so insistent on being nice to me, but I was bent on holding to my dislike of her.

"Okay," Eli finally chuckled, throwing her hands into her hair and walking away. As she reached my bedroom door, she turned over her shoulder and added:

"Let me know if you change your mind."

We'd meet again a few months later at a music festival. I attended Smokin' Grooves in March of that year with Katy and her friends, a group which, of course, included Eli. From that point on, her presence in my life was simply a given. She wasn't in school, and I had no idea what she did for work, but she seemed to always have a surplus of time to visit her high school friends.

It was only then, swooning to the sound of The Internet's *Wanna Be*, that I found myself open to getting to know her. I gazed at her as she stood by my side, hands stuffed inside her sweatshirt and big brown eyes hypnotized by Syd's swaying form, and I wondered.

Before I met Eli, my college love life was just a search to feel something; fruitless first date after fruitless first date; a string of drunken kisses and nameless hook-ups. The way that I treated my heart and my body at times bordered on self-harm in its recklessness. I think, at the time, I would have accepted love from anyone. Eli was just the first one to stick.

I should have known we weren't right for each other. She overused drugs frequently and, once, let her friends use the N-word in jest around me–but I had a blind spot for that kind of thing. I thought it was the intention that mattered. Time would show just how bad we were for each other, but I was persistent that I could make it work.

I didn't know it when we first met–at that time, I still considered Eli just another bead on the string of people who I dated and would eventually leave–but I would begin to choose this relationship over all else—her over my better instincts, over my pain, over my family. To be with her, I had to exclude my family from a large part of my life.

When I lost my first love, it was half-grown and just starting to bloom. Like with Eli, everything with us was always extreme; our love was constantly hanging on a precipice. I felt wheezy to think about it all.

I know now that I went to Eli with all my extremes because that is what I thought lovers were supposed to do. It wasn't fair, but a life-and-death kind of love was all I knew.

Despite her speeding, we arrived at Eli's family's home on that long drive up from Santa Barbara in one piece. I'd taken a long hit off of Eli's pen and let my worries about my mother and her lack of approval fade sometime between San Luis Obispo and San Jose.

Eli's dads were warm and welcoming, hugging me tightly as I entered their home, an unassuming white townhouse on a curved street of identical structures. They were both tall, beefy men who doted on their daughters ceaselessly and they quickly took me in as one of their own.

They seemed, to me, unreasonably worried about our safety at San Francisco Pride that year. The Supreme Court had overturned Roe v. Wade earlier that June. Eli's dads, among others, feared that a giant gathering of queers and weirdos in the heart of gay America would be appealing to some newly-empowered prolifer-type with a gun, if any such type existed.

But I had never been to San Francisco, or anywhere that far

north in California before. It seemed to me that in a city like that, we were untouchable. All of my problems were hours behind.

It was my first Pride festival. As Eli, her family, and I drove into the city, I gawked at the candy-colored houses angled off nearly vertical hills. It was colder than I'd imagined, the car windows frosty. When we arrived at the edge of San Francisco City Hall, Black and Brown couples spilled out of a subway entrance half-naked in shades of hot pink, blue, and yellow. To me, they were the very picture of queer liberation.

"Keep an eye on your phones and purses the whole time. And make sure you call us before you leave the venue," Mr. Hernandez said. He patted his daughters' heads as his husband, Frederik, dug through his purple fanny pack to receive cash for them. Despite the cold, there was a hot, stuffy feeling in the crowd at the entrance on Polk Street, vendors on either side of us waving bags of weed and rainbow t-shirts.

"Wait, where are you guys going?" Eli asked her dads as the two prepared to split off from us. The two stood pressed into each other's sides, engrossed in their phones.

"Leather Alley," Frederik said with a coy smile.

"And then maybe a bar?" his husband added on, watching him out of the corner of his eye.

"Only adults are allowed in those sections, sorry sweetie."

"Just sneak us in. You could buy us drinks," said Eli's teen sister, Ximena. When I first met Ximena and her friend Tali, I assumed they were much older than 17. Ximena was tall and thin with pale skin, lots of face piercings, and red streaks throughout her hair; Tali's were green. As we sped over the Golden Gate Bridge, she blasted the car with Lady Gaga and Russian rave music. She'd made it clear that without a high or buzz, what we did throughout the day was a moot point.

Mr. Hernandez just laughed. "There's so much to do; I'm sure you'll find something," he told us, scrolling through his phone.

"Go find one of the music stages," said Frederik. "There's a Latin one, oh, and Hip Hop."

Frederik wagged his eyebrow at me. Admittedly, the festival was the most Black and Brown people I had been around in months. I was sick of Santa Barbara EDM and surf rock, and the suggestion excited me. However, we lacked a map and soon found ourselves aimless.

For the first hour of the festival, we meandered through the streets, peeking our heads into booths selling jewelry and pride flags, past go-go dancers in speedos with dollar bills littered at their feet. The venue was contained to the few blocks of the city around the San Francisco Civic Center Plaza, a big patch of grass where a Main Stage for speakers and performers sat before the towering body of the Civic

Center.

Music pumped at every street corner, and voices boomed from the stands draped in white tarps to hide from the overcast sky. Everything drew my attention, and I was desperate to be a part of it all, but Ximena and Tali were bored and expressed it loudly.

"Give me your Stiiizy." Ximena held out her hand to her sister as we stopped at the end of a long block.

Eli pulled the purple vape pen from her pocket, and her sister took a long draw, blowing it up above our heads in a neat ring. Since we arrived, Ximena had one singular goal: to find booze. None of us were twenty-one yet, so her plan was to find some sweet, compassionate-seeming person in line to buy drinks for us.

"Maybe that one," Ximena said, pointing to an older woman waiting to buy a drink. The bar was on the edge of the sidewalk, a line of people spilling into the street for her to choose from. This woman was graying but sweet-seeming in her bumblebee-themed outfit.

"No, she looks too old. She'll feel responsible," Tali told her.

Eli scanned the crowd with an interrogative gaze. "I don't know," she said. "She looks cool."

"Do you really need to drink that badly?" I held my arms crossed tightly across my chest.

Ximena rolled her eyes, "I'm going to try."

She grabbed her friend's arm and kneaded her way through

the crowd.

Eli's elbow nudged my side. "Loosen up," she said, pulling out her phone to take selfies. I held my lips together.

"Here, give me," I said. I took Eli's phone and knelt down to get a better angle of her pink, blue, and purple outfit. She fanned out a pride flag the size of a cape behind her and smiled.

"Why are you against Ximena getting drinks?" Eli asked me between poses. "It's not like we're going get in trouble." She pointed to a cop standing a few feet away.

I didn't really have an answer for her. Every moment that we'd spent with her sister, we'd done so drunk or high or looking to get drunk or high. I was finding it exhausting. In fact, it was becoming concerning to me just how much time Eli spent inebriated.

I could tell that her sister didn't like me just yet; I was too uptight, and she made me feel too uncool. But I couldn't say that. Instead, I just told Eli that it didn't seem like a good use of our time.

Down the street, a crowd formed in front of a Latin band. I watched them dance and sway in couples, yelling exuberantly.

"C'mon, don't you want to go dance or something?" I asked Eli, pulling her body towards me. I swayed our bodies to and fro with the music, our hips syncing in rhythm. Eli pressed her face into my neck, and her warmth made me feel good again.

"Let's go, just for a second," I whispered in her ear. "They'll be fine."

Eli laughed but pulled away from my touch. "Just wait for a second."

She looked over my shoulder.

"Wait, where'd they go?"

In the crowd, Ximena and Tali were nowhere to be seen.

"Fuck," Eli cursed, pulling out her phone to text Ximena. I stood on the street corner, waiting for one of their red or green heads to pop up, while Eli paced and stared at her phone screen. No response came.

"Fuck it, come on," Eli pulled me down the street. "We have to find her."

We traced our way back through the festival, down the line of bar carts, past the Latin stage and the go-go dancers across the Civic Center, until we were back at the entrance facing Polk Street.

"Let's look for the other stages; I bet she ended up somewhere near one of them."

Left of the Main Stage, I could hear bass pumping from a sparsely-lined alleyway.

"Wait, I think that's the Hip Hop stage," I said, speeding up. "Maybe she's there?"

Eli shrugged, not hopeful but willing to look anywhere. I grabbed her hand and peeked down the alley. I made out the outline of a large crowd when a man in full-body fishnets dashed past us. Then, two women holding tight to each other who struggled to run in their high heels, stumbling like baby deer, their faces panicked.

The music trailing towards us stopped. A few more people scattered past us, and I froze for only a second, meeting Eli's panicked eyes. I grabbed her arm and we ran towards the Plaza, where a stampede of people fled the stage.

The crowds lounging on the Plaza grass stood up in shifts, alert. Some began to run. Others pelted questions as we ran, like "What's happening?" and "What's going on?"

I could only wheeze out: "I don't know."

No one knew.

Eli and I ran to the far right side of the Plaza, where we crouched behind a taco trunk. I heaved deep breaths into my burning lungs, searching across the Plaza lawn for any sign of a familiar face.

"She won't pick up. Why won't she pick up?" Eli banged her phone against the wall in frustration. Still, there was no sign of Ximena.

In front of the Civic Center, a drag queen in a towering white wig was escorted off the stage, the screens around her going dark. The music around us quieted as a voice crackled through the loudspeakers.

"Please, remain calm," the voice ordered.

Someone was working to fix things, they told us. They said we just had to remain calm.

I could hear heavy footsteps, like horses trotting, and a lot of heavy breathing, but no gunshots or screaming. Next to me, a large woman with bantu knots placed her hand on my arm.

"It's gonna be alright," she said to me. Her eyes were a deep brown, almost black, and shiny like marbles. They pleaded with me, trying to communicate some assurance words couldn't. "We're all going be alright, okay?"

I sank to the floor and held in my tears as Eli phoned her dads and her sister over and over again. I wondered if I should say a prayer.

"Dad? Dad?" Eli hissed into her phone.

The entire plaza had gone silent, waiting.

"Where are you?" I could hear Mr. Hernandez' booming voice on the other end of the call.

"We're by the lawn," Eli whispered. "In front of the stage."

"Lawn? Which lawn? Wait, what did you say? Where's Ximena?"

Around us, every cart and booth had been abandoned, and half of the people in attendance had filtered out of the venue. Everyone else was asking the people around them what happened. What was going on? No one had a clear answer, but the general consensus was that we were safe. No one was coming to kill us. We were safe.

"Is that Ximena?"

A few feet in front of us, squatting behind a table of unwatched drinks, I saw them: Ximena, Tali, and two boys we hadn't met.

"What is she doing?" I asked.

Eli laughed, relieved. Ximena and her friend had found some boys, and now they were trying to steal more drinks in the chaos.

Eli grabbed her sister by the arm. "Come on, Ximena. We need to leave."

"Why?" Ximena scoffed. "Nothing's happening. We're *fine*."

I still hadn't come down from the fear that took over me in the alleyway. My eyes flitted from Ximena to Eli, to the woman returning to the booth, to the alleyway across the Plaza, to the crowds of people making their way out.

I tugged on Eli's arm, feeling like a child. "Can we please go?"

"I just want to get another drink first," Ximena said.

My body felt antsy and erratic. "No. I'm not staying."

I walked off without checking to see if Eli was following, though I knew she would eventually.

I didn't really know where I was going. With Eli trailing behind, I struggled to navigate the cityscape to find our meetup spot. I realized for the first time that day that I had no idea where I was, in the city, or in the world. That was the farthest I had ever been from home. Santa Barbara was about seven hours away by then, and my real home—my parents and my sister—about nine hours away. The fear within me only magnified.

We found the festival entrance on Polk Street, but there was no sign of Mr. Hernandez or Frederik. While Eli and I held each other to fight off the cold, I watched swaths of people descend down to the BART as police squads arrived at the venue by the dozens—fire trucks, police vans, and at least twenty cycles. We stood shivering in the foggy San Francisco cold for five, ten, fifteen, twenty-five, thirty minutes until Eli got a call from her stepdad.

"Uh-uh. You're where? How long. *Where?*"

Frederik's arm waved at us above the heads of the police cycles, and we ran across the street to meet them. With them were Ximena and Tali, giddy inside their hoodies.

Frederik's face dripped with tears as he swallowed Eli in his arms. He pulled me into a crushing hug next as Mr. Hernandez began rushing us away.

"Oh God, we were so worried about you! Where were you guys? What happened?"

I walked quickly with her dads, retelling the tale again while Eli fell behind with her sister.

"Where were you guys when we left before you?" Eli asked her sister.

"We got the lady to buy us drinks," said Ximena. "What do you mean?"

The girls laughed, and I huddled into my jacket. I wanted to feel calm and relieved, to laugh at the situation, but for some reason I just couldn't.

When we got back to Eli's house, we found out that there were no shooting or bomb threats that day like we had assumed. I found out from Twitter, watching a video from under the covers of Eli's bed, freshly showered and scrubbed raw: there was a fight that started at the Hip Hop stage, and an idiot who decided pepper spray was the solution. People scattered from the scene, and that fear butterflied.

"So there was no reason for us to run?" Eli scoffed.

"There could have been." Something in me needed to insist this.

"But there wasn't."

I said nothing back. How was she so fine?

"I'm gonna call my mom, okay?"

Eli shrugged and returned to her phone, curled away from me but close enough to hear the call. I turned the other way and listened to the line ring. I willed my mom to pick up.

"Hello?" Relief was the scratchy sound of my mother's voice on the other end of the line.

"Hi, Mommy?" I gasped. "I'm at Eli's—I'm at my girlfriend's house. We got here yesterday. I'm safe."

"Oh, that's good," my mom said. She sounded genuinely relieved.

I waited for her to say something, anything, about what she was thinking about Eli. But for once, she didn't. It was like she was holding her tongue, but about what, I didn't know.

"We just got back from Pride, actually."

"Well, how was it?"

"It was.. it was fine. Good. I mean we drove all the way to San Francisco, and then we had to park and take an Uber there, but they took us to the wrong location. The Uber driver thought we were going to a building called P.R.I.D.E. I think it was some kind of metal shop? Oh, and I saw the outside of that big domed museum. It was really beautiful, except for some man that was on the lawn dancing in a thong."

"Well, you wanted to go to San Francisco," my mom snickered, imagining the undulating man. "Those are your people."

"I think he was doing some kind of yoga?" I laughed. "But, um, something did happen at the Pride."

My mom paused. "Oh?"

I didn't quite know how to tell her what had happened. I didn't want her to live in fear of what would happen to me as

I ventured further and further out into a world she fully didn't understand. I didn't understand it either.

"Yeah. It was nothing, really. Just, like, there were people running from one of the stages, and some things got shut down. I guess they thought somebody had a gun or something. But they didn't," I rushed to add on the last part.

Another pause. "Are you okay?" she asked.

"Yeah, I think so. We are."

She sounded out of breath. "Well, I'm glad you two are okay."

"Yeah, me too," I said, tears welling in my eyes. "Mommy, I love you."

I hoped that was enough to say everything that went unsaid: that I was sorry and that I missed her and I wished things were good enough between us that we could be together. More than anything in the world, when nothing around me felt safe, she was the one I wanted to be with. But I couldn't say that; something, pride perhaps, wouldn't let me.

"I love you too. And be safe over there, please."

I wondered what went unsaid in her words.

"I know. I will."

I hung up the phone and rolled over into Eli's arms, pressing my wet eyes into her chest. She wrapped her arms around me but, somehow, they felt frail and weak, so I clutched her harder to compensate.

"Are you okay?" Eli asked.

I was happy to be alive and glad to be with someone I loved, but I desperately wanted to be somewhere that felt like home. It was hard to admit that I wanted what I was running from.

"Yeah."

I decided it was better to hold it all in. I didn't know what to say or how to say it, so it was better if I said nothing at all. Really, a large part of me still felt like I needed to run. But I couldn't run any further than I already had. All I could do was cling closer to her.

Not long after the trip, I started to have anxiety attacks again. It was that fearful, trembling feeling that'd overcome me behind the abandoned truck at Pride, only now I knew how to name it. Now, they came all the time.

When I left Eli's house after our Pride trip, I quickly began to spiral. The fear in my body translated into endless crying and a deep depression. Without her, most days, I was unable to leave my bed, like I couldn't cope or sooth on my own.

Then, when we finally did meet again, I spent our time together on my toes, so high I was anxiously awaiting a fall. When we were good, we were each other's reasons for living; when we were bad, it felt like the world ceased to turn.

The longer we stayed together, the more we fought over money, responsibilities, friends, family, and sex. Things always seemed to end in us hurting each other or ourselves. Like our first breakup. My 20th birthday. The first trip to meet my parents. Our second breakup.

When Eli got upset with me, she would smoke herself into oblivion and go silent, turning away from me and not speaking for hours. I'd sit in that silence, itching until it all burst, and I went ballistic, threatening to leave. Eventually we'd make up, and then it'd start all over again.

When my mom got an inkling that things weren't quite right, she referred me to a therapist from the clinic she saw in Long Beach. I brushed her off. Why would I try therapy again when the last experience ended so badly?

I struggled to talk about my anxiety, my inability to socialize, or eat, or get out of bed, and the urge to hurt myself again. I even struggled to talk about Eli. Somehow, the inability to talk about my relationship with my family had morphed into an inability to talk about my relationship, period.

To talk about the relationship negatively, the relationship I had so badly wanted, felt like treason. It was as if I didn't truly accept all of Eli's apologies and promises to get better. And I did want to believe those things.

Everything took a turn for the worst, however, when my Uncle died.

My Uncle Paul had been sick throughout the course of our relationship. I never fully knew how serious it was, but part of me had a feeling; I just chose to ignore it. It was a nagging feeling in the back of my mind; a reminder that my family as I knew it could fall apart at any moment.

Half a year into the relationship, during the fall quarter of my junior year at UC Santa Barbara, it finally happened.

I didn't know how to cope with death, so I pushed it off. I took advantage of all that was around me and I drank, and smoked, and partied until I couldn't feel anything anymore. I felt like something had broken within me. To Eli though, nothing in the world had changed.

That year, on Thanksgiving, a month after my uncle had passed, my mother met Eli for the first time. This time, Eli was coming to stay with my family. Introducing her to them was part of my plan to patch all the pain of the past few months over, but we struggled to get through a single day without fighting.

A few hours before all my relatives were meant to arrive, my mother stood in the kitchen in an apricot housedress, basting a large turkey, a spread of foiled containers lining the countertops. Her curly hair stuck to the sweat on her face and she blew it away, meeting my eyes. I stood in the doorway, tears rolling down my cheeks. My hands tugged at the sleeves of my sweater, pulled over my forearms.

I said nothing and went into her open arms.

"Do you want me to talk to her?" she asked. I shook my head. My mother couldn't fix my relationship.

She held me for a moment, smelling of warm lily petals and salty brine. When she pulled me back, I did not expect the stony look in her eyes. My mother held me by the shoulders as she spoke to me.

"Maya, this doesn't have to be your forever. Some people are in your life for a season, a reason, or a lifetime."

It sounded cheesy, but I knew she was serious.

I felt suddenly fragile and pulled away. I knew she could see right through us. My mother was no fool.

I turned my head so she could no longer see the tears in my eyes. "Please, don't say that."

My mother crossed her arms over her chest. "Your grandparents are going to be here soon. You gotta ask yourself what really matters."

At dinner, we all pretended everything was alright. Eli arrived late, which only made coming out to my grandparents more awkward. But unlike the million catastrophes I'd imagined of this moment over the years, no one said a word. They smiled and asked about school and Eli's job like having her there wasn't entirely out of the ordinary. I wasn't a child anymore; my decisions were mine alone and mine to live with.

It was half past nine in my parent's house and my bedroom was dark, the orange glow of LED lights surrounding my bed. Everyone else in the house had gone to bed, and Eli and I lay on top of my bedspread, half-awake, half-asleep. It was a miracle that my mother let us sleep in the same room, but she seemed to be warming up to the idea of having Eli here, or else growing more lenient. Still, the door was split open. As per her request, it was never to remain closed with both of us inside.

With my head on Eli's chest, rising and falling to the rhythm of her breath, I couldn't find calm. I still had a nagging, trembling feeling inside of me; that trait I inherited from my mother that wouldn't allow me to let things go. Undressed from the day's activities, I wore a pair of pajama bottoms I'd found in my old dresser and a white tank top, my arms bare. In the orange glow, I could make out the faint, white lines that scarred my left forearm. I traced my finger across the row of them, like lines of empty sheet music, to the crease of my elbow where one mark scabbed, the brown crust just starting to peel. Maybe certain things couldn't just be swept under the rug.

I stood up and closed the door. Eli sat up on my bed, her torso lifted up on her elbows.

"What's up?" she said.

I stood with my back pressed to the door.

"What happened this morning?" I asked.

Eli shrugged. "I don't know what you mean." Her eyes were blank and expressionless. I didn't know how she could brush past the things that bothered her so easily.

"Yes, you do," I hissed. "You knew my whole family was out there, and you shut down completely." I hoped to keep my volume low enough that no one else in the house would hear me, but it was difficult to mask my growing outrage.

"You wouldn't come out. You wouldn't say 'hi'. You wouldn't even speak to me. I bring you here to meet my entire family and you spend the morning ignoring me. Ignoring *them*.

Do you know how embarrassing that was? To have to go to my grandparents–who I'm coming out to for the *first time*–and make up some excuse of why my girlfriend refused to greet them? Why would you do that?"

Eli looked out my bedroom window, eyes glazed over like she was watching something far in the distance. My voice echoed faintly off the walls and I breathed in deeply, trying to calm myself. I raised my eyebrows in gesture, waiting for a response; some kind of explanation.

"Really, nothing?" My voice squeaked. Beneath the guilt and the anger, what I really felt was weak; desperate and isolated. My relationship was falling apart in front of me and I didn't know how to fix it. I couldn't reach out to anyone about it. I felt like I was in it alone.

I took her hands into mine and tried to meet her eyes, pleading.

"I just couldn't do it," Eli whispered.

"Do what?" I asked, not understanding.

"Your family, they were so nice, but I just–" Eli's mouth screwed up as she tried to find the right words to say.

"Seeing your mom and how she acts with you–it made me think about my mom, I guess. She even reminds me of her a bit. Not the bad parts, I mean. The good parts, when she still acted like a mom.

It just makes me miss her in some weird way. But I don't want to miss her. God–I mean, *fuck* her. She's barely a mother and she doesn't deserve to be missed! She's done so much fucked up shit and I just–" Eli stopped, breathing heavily. She scrunched her nose and looked up to the ceiling, tears rising in her eyes.

"I don't know," she said.

The longer I got to know Eli, the more I realized that what I was drawn to in her was the same thing that resided in me. Deep inside we were both just hurt little girls looking for comfort. I didn't know if she had the space to care for me in the way I needed to be cared for, but in times like this, caring for her felt like enough.

I wrapped my arms around Eli, pulling her head to my chest. We said nothing for a long time while I closed my eyes and listened to the sound of her heartbeat and the cars passing by outside. The smell of her sweat was sweet and musky, the top of her head smooth like silk beneath my fingers.

Then, Eli's hand cupped my face and she kissed me. It was aggressive, the kiss, as her arm winded behind my waist and fingers pressed into my spine.

I kissed back, though I wasn't sure it was what I wanted. Inside me, too many different emotions were clashing, begging for my attention; grief, sorrow, anger, pity, sympathy, love, resentment. For once, sex didn't feel like the right answer.

As her head began to lower down my neck, I lifted her chin and kissed her lips, softly.

"I'm fine," I said. "You don't have to."

"It's okay, I want to," she said, and continued to kiss her way down my torso.

"No, Eli," I chuckled, her lip tickling my stomach. "I mean it,

I'm fine."

She didn't stop. Her fingers sunk into my hips as she pulled me closer. I gasped, my body frozen as the walls of my teenage bedroom closed in around me.

"Stop," I said, but she didn't; not quickly enough. "Eli, stop!"

I forced her shoulders away from me and pulled my legs towards my stomach. Eli pushed her body back, eyes wide.

We sat on opposite ends of the bed, legs curled to our chests like children. I held my forearms in my hands, thumbs pressing deeply into the skin as I watched her from the corner of my eye. She would not look at me.

"Will you say something?" I said.

I wanted her to say *I'm sorry*. I wanted her to hold me.

When I realized she wouldn't, I laid down facing the wall. I heard her stand up and open the bedroom door. Then, from afar, the front door opened and slammed shut.

I closed my eyes and willed myself to sleep.

As they did every time I left home, my father kissed me on my forehead, and my mother held back tears as she held me one last time. I breathed in her scent and prayed that its memory would not leave me so soon. I knew, because my sister told me so, that my mom cried each time I left, only waiting for me to disappear around the corner of our street before she let the tears fall. For the first time in a very long time, as our home shrunk into the corner of Eli's car window, I let myself cry too.

My girlfriend and I's relationship ended the day of our one-year anniversary. What I remember most clearly is struggling to hold her upright in the shower of my college apartment. Eli's short frame shivered against me as the steam rose from her skin, vibrant pink from the heat and yet so pale she seemed nearly dead. Her head hung against my shoulder, inky strands clinging to her face. I ran my fingers through them, but she wouldn't open her eyes. Her body against mine felt like a heartbeat: warm and soft, fragile.

I felt like if I let her go for even a second, she would disappear, and I would be left with nothing.

It happened on the curve of the Ventura highway. The morning after our last fight, Eli no longer wanted to go on the trip I'd planned. She said it would just be a waste of money and energy. Why couldn't we just stay in? Why couldn't that be enough?

It was my punishment for pushing so relentlessly for the perfect anniversary trip. I didn't really even want it for us. What I wanted was to prove that this relationship could be everything I needed it would be. I needed the expensive hotel and perfect anniversary story to prove that I'd made the right choice; to my mother, who knew we were wrong for each other the moment they met; to my grandmother, who refused to remember her name; to my father who would still only call her my friend. But mostly to myself, as I still believed this relationship would make me complete.

As we drove off from my apartment, I kissed Eli's hand and held it in mine. I thought to myself, *if I love her hard enough, I can make this all better.*

Two hours later, a swift jolt and the ear-splitting screech of crunching metal and glass woke me from my sleep.

"Fuck. Fuck, fuck, fuck!" Eli was screaming, tears bubbling in the corners of her eyes. Her hands were covered in little cuts, and blood gushed from her top lip and gums. Above my head, her car's windshield was splintered like a spiderweb.

How many times had I let her drive around in that car, kissed her in that car, screamed and cried in that car, only to see it totaled in the middle of a busy freeway–hood was folded up like a piece of tinfoil?

Time slowed around me like Jell-O. I could see Eli through the cracked windshield, fragments of her with her head in her hands, pacing in front of all that smoke and debris. I pushed myself out of the passenger seat, my arms and legs stiff, and flattened myself against the side of the car facing the busy highway.

It was freezing cold and loud. Each car that skidded by

vibrated in my bones. The owners of the Tesla she'd crashed into looked at us both without an idea of what to do. Their car was merely dented. Eli would have to pay for that later.

I tucked myself into the backseat of the car, terrified of the highway rushing around me. Inside, it smelled like chemicals, and I choked on them.

I knew then that it was over. Without a car, our long-distance visits would simply end, and after those next few days, I would likely never see Eli again. But in the moment, that was too heavy a thought. For that night, I focused on lathering her hair with shampoo and washing the smoke from it, picking out pieces of shattered glass with my pruned fingertips.

For the next few days, I would pet her head and coax her out of bed. I would hold her up in the shower and scrub her back. I would try not to remember that it was our anniversary.

At the end of our anniversary trip, Eli caught a ride back home from my roommate and left the BMW's bones parked in front of my apartment. She gathered all that was left from her car: old ID cards, several pairs of sneakers, and a Ziploc bag of shrooms.

We clung to each other and cried in a familiar way in the driveway. Then, we said goodbye. That was the last time I ever held her.

When the car had driven off, I crawled back into the backseat of Eli's BMW and held my knees to my chest, waiting. I wanted to feel something; smell some familiar scent, feel some familiar feeling. A comforting warmth. Home.

There was nothing left in that car but metal scraps and empty memories.

Death and Ancestors

As a child, grief was stored in my father's bedroom. It was the thickness of incense sticks burning in a glass cup, and a wall of old photographs and funeral pamphlets that stretched from the floor to the ceiling: his wall of ancestors.

I believe that he prayed to them and spoke to them. Most of the Black Christians I have known do not seriously believe in witchcraft, magic, or voodoo, yet our culture has so many spiritual practices that predate Christianity. They persist despite it; seep into us, and make a habit of things others can't understand.

It's why we make collard greens and black-eyed peas for luck on New Year's Day and open windows to let out spirits we supposedly don't believe in; why we don't let young girls put their purses on the floor; why the broom my mother and father jumped at their wedding still hung on my living room wall.

For me, religion has always been the one-room church in Santa Monica where my father and his siblings were raised. For years, I had told myself that it was that church that had separated me from my family. I remembered my Uncle Ramon, our pastor, telling the congregation that his brother, who liked men, was condemned to hell. That day, I excused myself to the bathroom as I couldn't keep myself from crying. I was only 13, but I told myself that I would never willingly step foot in that church again.

As years passed, I did my best to make good on that promise. By the time I returned from college, the church hardly felt mine to claim anymore. I only ever visited our church when it was time for a funeral. The first was my Grandad's. Then Auntie Cookie's. Then Uncle Paul's. Though the church was hardly mine to claim anymore, it was still where I came to lay our dead to rest. It brought us together for better or for worse.

My whole family–grandparents, aunts, and uncles, as well as distant cousins and family friends–gathered in the space for mourning time and time again. It was my Grandma Ruby's soft, soulful mezzo-soprano rising above the church pews in hymn. It was Sunday dinners in the church classroom, trying to guess whose sweet potato pie was on the menu and if it was store-bought or homemade. Those were the moments when I truly felt something; I just didn't have the words for it. It was all too complicated.

For my father—the eclectic history buff—religion and mysticism often became one. He was a high school teacher of history and ethnic studies who'd devoted several years to painting a giant map of the world onto his classroom wall, complete with drawings of indigenous artifacts and flags. His classroom was a museum, filled with wooden busts, and African drums and finger instruments. My dad was also known to get into theological debates with his brother, our pastor. In my atheistic, rebellious phase, I liked the way that he poked holes in the logic of the Bible and the timeline of Christ. I felt satisfied in my belief in nothing. As I got older, though, it was his wall of ancestors that stuck with me the most.

I remember the day I walked into my father's room and saw my Grandad's funeral pamphlet, newly added to the wall. Not his father, but my mother's father. After my Grandad passed when I was 10, it felt like our whole house went through a heavy depression. I suppose it was mostly my mother's to bear, but nonetheless I felt it well into my teen years.

It was my dad who took us outside to the stream behind Grandad's funeral home and told us not to cry when my mother could barely speak and did not want to be touched.

I didn't know at the time what kind of complicated relationship my mother had with her father; I just knew that he was my Grandma's husband and my Grandad. He had the arms of a sailor—big and covered in tattoos—that he'd use to swing me around as a child. He taught my sister and I to fish; the right kind of bait to use and how to cast the rod. He once even taught me that when the bad sitcoms we watched on Disney Channel used laugh tracks, it was because their joke really wasn't that funny, and they wanted to convince us otherwise. Sometimes, he'd leave for a long time on fishing trips, but he'd always come back. He'd be sitting on the couch with a TV table and whatever my grandma cooked for dinner, ready to crack a joke or dispel wisdom.

One day, when I was 10, my mom took my sister and I out for frozen yogurt after school and sat us down at our dining room table, me on her lap and Margot leaning over us. This was in the rented house we lived in while I was in middle school that none of us really liked. It had odd brown carpeting and the stain of cat piss on the dining room wall behind where we sat for dinner. It was the house where we got robbed one day—with nothing much to steal besides Daddy's camera that held a bulk of home videos and my mother's nice gold jewelry. And it was where Mommy told us that Grandad had cancer.

It could have been weeks or months after that that she sat us down in her bedroom and let us know that Grandad was dead.

When my mom lost her father, she became the first model for

grief I had. I watched that sadness fester inside her, turning everything in that house dark. I was too young to really understand all that death had changed around me. Instead, I felt the displacement deep within, an emptiness that grew without explanation or announcement over the next few years.

I never got to know my Grandad as an adult or even a teenager. To me, he was an unfinished painting, splashes of color over a rough sketch with the white of the paper always peeking through.

Yet, for years, I couldn't listen to songs that had played at his funeral. Bill Withers, *Just the Two of Us*, and *As* by Stevie Wonder stuck with me the most. Just the first few notes of *As* could bring me to tears–unbearable, choking tears. The feelings songs can bring out of people have always had a spiritual quality to me. In the church I grew up in, we never sang with a choir. We were to lift up our voices in praise of God so that my tiny voice meant something.

I could not sing those songs.

During college, after Uncle Paul had passed, I came back to the memory of my grandfather's death often. At age 11, I walked into my father's room and saw my Grandad's funeral pamphlet on his wall among my great aunts and great grandparents in orange-tinged and black and white photos. He was the first face I recognized. His voice was the only one I could still hear in my head if I focused hard enough.

I often went into my father's room to stare at the wall when he was not home. If I spoke to my grandfather, I would always scurry out after. I felt that if someone caught me and saw me, then it would be less real.

I know that my father added him to the wall for us. To give a way to grieve. To keep him alive.

When I first moved into my college apartment, I put up three portraits. One was of my sister and I, taken just before I left home. The second was of my parents, my mother smiling with her nose scrunched up the way I so often do now. The third was a Johnson family portrait, taken the last Fourth of July we celebrated before I left home. It was the last photo taken of all us: Grandma and Grandpa; all seven of their children, their partners and children and dogs. We all stood or sat beneath my Aunt's trellis of her backyard in Inglewood.

Only one person was missing from the photo: my Uncle Paul. He was standing on the edge of the trellis, cut out of the frame of my perfect 4x4 print.

It was as if he fell from the photo.

It began one night as I left work in October of my junior year, starting out the semester with a familiarly homesick lull.

I was just getting started at my new job. I left the restaurant in a slump of flour and exhaustion when I got a call from my dad. At this new job, my parents never knew when I was working. My shifts could end at one in the morning or three in the afternoon, and so they started every call with the same script:

"Hey love–are you busy?"

I told my dad that I was out of work and continued walking home, past the Starbucks storefront glowing in green neon light. His voice sounded different than usual: sniffly and strained. I didn't know my father to be a man who often cried.

"You know, Uncle Paul has been in the hospital again."

Yes, I knew, I told him. Perhaps I had been too caught up in my own bullshit again to pay close enough attention, though. I knew that Uncle Paul had been in and out of the hospital since the beginning of summer.

The last time I'd seen him was that June, when he had come to pick me up from Los Angeles Union Station to take me out to lunch. He didn't say why he had, there was no special occasion. He just wanted to see me.

When he first arrived, he seemed boisterous as ever, cracking jokes and making conversation with strangers in line as I knew him to do. It wasn't until we left the restaurant that I noticed his skin was fading in color, and the smile lines on his face seemed deeper than before.

From the start, he had kept his energy levels up for me, made that long drive from Riverside to Union Station; a drive so long in his condition that I still didn't know how to comprehend it. On our way back, he talked of the expectations everyone had of him and how they were weighing on him in those days. I didn't realize that he was dying.

Us Johnsons always seemed to bounce back. It would be a slow recovery, but a recovery nonetheless.

"Uncle Paul," my dad said slowly. "He–he's passed."

Something left my body. My legs went weak, so I gripped the ramp to stay upright.

"No. No, I thought he was getting better. That's why you waited to tell me that he was back in the hospital, why I didn't go home."

His stint in the hospital was supposed to be just the next in a series of surgeries from which he would recover. Until that moment, I hadn't even begun to entertain the possibility of death.

I don't think I ever really left that night, breathless, holding myself up against a ramp rail. Later that night, I picked up my phone to call Eli, but I didn't know what say to her. I curled up alone in my busy apartment and cried myself to sleep from grief and guilt and wondered why I hadn't been home.

I felt so alone at school, grieving in an apartment of five girls, none of whom really knew me or could support me. My family was miles and miles away. I felt for the first time that need for something higher. I wanted, needed, to see higher coincidences. I began to collect little rituals like my father, hanging portraits on my wall and burning incense sticks, hoping the smell would heal me.

I thought of speaking to my father's wall and understood his need to have them there, to always see them, so they didn't just disappear. I wanted to remember it all. To hold onto them all.

When I lost my uncle, he had become one of my favorite people. He was the one that introduced me to my favorite movie, *The Wiz*. When I was much younger, we would watch it each time he visited, at my request, so I could hear Diana Ross sing: "When I think of home.." in that sweet gospel tone of hers. It reminded me of my grandmother.

He was the one who made my favorite food: slow-cooked, dry-rub pork ribs. When he barbequed, he'd have to make pounds of them, portioned out into metal tins covered in foil that got distributed to everyone he knew, bought and fought over.

When I was a scrawny middle-school student, stretched-out like a green bean, Uncle Paul tried to get me to join his basketball team, and drove me out into Los Angeles to awkwardly shoot balls. It's because of him that I passed that unit in PE.

"Just aim for the backboard," he told me.

In high school, he took my sister and me to our first and only baseball game in Dodger Stadium. Uncle Paul bought tickets for us and his nephew and took us all over L.A. from Watts to Union Station. He was the first one to ever walk me through Union Station all those years ago. It was, to me, so breathtakingly grand and bustling, like taking a big step into some unknown new start.

The last time I saw him, my Uncle Paul took me to get French-dipped sandwiches and pie at the same restaurant we went to on Dodgers Day. As I knew him to do, he talked to just about anyone he could in line, even the cops behind us. I'd always considered myself as shy and sheltered, but Uncle Paul made everyone feel like they could talk to him.

I told him about my girlfriend that day, one of the first ones in my family that I came out to. I thought the way he reacted to this new bit of information about me was funny, telling me stories of his player days in high school as if I was suddenly just a nephew to him.

He was one of the funniest people I knew, even though all my uncles are very funny. They each have their own type of funny, and Uncle Paul was a mean type of funny. But, he was a good enough man that he could shit-talk anyone within spitting distance and still be overwhelmingly beloved. For example, his nickname for my mom was Auntie shit. When she was on the phone with him, I'd always hear her howling with laughter from her room. If I remember the story correctly, I think he might have been the reason my parents met. It was at one of his parties, where my Mom's friends knew Paul, because *everyone* knew and loved Paul.

I wondered what it meant now that my uncle Paul was an ancestor too. He was always godly in a way. He knew everyone and how to do everything. His funeral was a large gathering at the church, each wooden pew filled and huge bouquets scattered at the pulpit. His basketball team held another celebration for him afterward. I was far from the only one who loved and missed him and thought of him daily.

I thought of him when I cooked and when I straightened the portraits on my wall. I thought of him when my mom laughed on the phone with my uncles and when my dad barbequed in the backyard. And I thought of him every time I walked through L.A. Union Station, finally heading home again. I thought of him as he stopped by the communal piano, bathed in that angelic, reverberating sound, cracking jokes at the scruffy man singing along to Stevie Wonder.

Though I can't be sure, my brain liked to believe the song was *As*, simply for my own sense of something higher, though it was likely something more upbeat like *Superstition* or *Isn't She Lovely*. Instead, I liked to remember it as if it was plucked from a hymn book on the back of the church's old wooden pews. I wished I could still hear it, let the sound of his humming repeat on:

> *(Until the trees and seas just up and fly away) always,*
>
> *(Until the day that eight times eight times eight is four) always,*
>
> *(Until the day that is the day that are no more)*

Always.

Home

      In June of my junior year–several months after my relationship had ended and nearly a year since Uncle Paul had passed—I received grant money through my university to attend the Santa Barbara Writers Conference with a few of my classmates. Each year the SBWC covered the cost of attendance for a few lucky students within my writing program.

      "Don't miss a chance to rub elbows with well-known authors and publishing professions!" my program advisor had emailed. Refocusing on my writing and my career felt like the perfect thing to take my mind off of the past few months.

      When my uncle died, my family called on me endlessly to check in on how I was doing–my mother, my father, my sister, even my grandmother–and I just told them that I was fine, over and over again. I did not want to face how I felt and I did not want to cry again.

When I broke up with Eli half a year later, I simply didn't tell my family the relationship had ended.

The last phone call I'd had with my mother–a week before the conference–the topic did not come up. We talked about school and about the grant and discussed whether or not I was coming home for the Fourth of July. I just didn't mention it. I wasn't sure she would care.

I thought, *it'll come up in conversation at some point.* Until then, I was fine braving the grief of that relationship on my own.

I did anything I could that summer to distract myself from the fact that I was alone once again. At times, being with Eli had felt just as lonely as being single, but at least she was there. Without her I did not know who I would call on when things felt dark or heavy. I simply had to find ways to cope and distract myself on my own.

The fiction workshop that I attended on the second day of the Santa Barbara Writers Conference was held in a back room of Santa Barbara's Mar Monte Hotel, through many strange, twisting staircases and carpeted halls. Passing row after row of doors where women bussed carts of dirty white sheets, I felt I should not be there.

The spanish-colonial style of downtown Santa Barbara had

always reminded me of the missions my classmates and I had visited on field trips. Mission field trips were a staple of growing up in Southern California.

To bask in the glory of what Spanish settlers had accomplished through subjugation and forced labor was vital to our educational development. The arched white stucco and red tiling made me feel like I was standing in an artifact of history; a conquest won by someone else.

In the back halls of the hotel, however, there was no majesty. In the dimly lit hall where I stood, the greenish blue carpet looked dirty and the air smelled stale. I checked my phone impulsively for the fifth time that hour: "No new notifications," it read. In another life, I would have texted Eli each nervous thought and smart aleck comment that was passing through my head. Instead, I pushed the device to the bottom of my tote bag and told myself not to pick it up again.

By the time I found the room my workshop was held in–down the stale hall and past the ice machine, right across from the janitor's closet–my group of writers had already introduced themselves and begun to read. Eight pairs of eyes met me as I pushed the heavy wooden door open.

A full-length mirror hung from the wall across from me and reflected my appearance; my hunched shoulders and skinny legs sprouting out of the tan Calvin Klein wrap dress I'd thrifted with matching heeled loafers. I waved a shy "hello" to the group.

"Sorry," I said. "I had trouble finding the room."

The small hotel room had no bed. There were couches pressed along each wall, which would have made the space feel cramped if not for a large bay window that hung open across from where I stood. In the center of the room, a set of folding chairs were arranged in a circle around my instructor. She was a round-faced white woman named Lorelai who appeared to be in her late seventies.

I'd picked Lorelai's workshop, "Discovering your Secret Story", out of a list of similarly cheesy names—"The Art of the Character," "Writing as a Craft," —because I found her portrait in the SBWC brochure to be comforting. The brochure pictured her with her head resting on her hand, silver strands falling over her fingers as she gazed forward with kind, gentle eyes. I let the door to the hotel room fall closed and her gentle eyes met mine. She smiled, gesturing towards an empty seat between a curly-haired boy who looked to be around my age and an older man reading from a printed manuscript on his lap.

Wind flapped through the curtains of the big bay window that overlooked the beach two floors below us. It made the room appear to breathe.

"Well, uh, I finished this memoir about twelve years ago,"

the old man said. He acknowledged me with a small nod as I lowered myself down next to him. He was nearly bald, with patches of gray sprouting up at odd spots on his head, and spoke with a hint of a Southern accent.

"The book's been published for some time now," he said. "Got a lot of good reviews, too. I'm still just looking for some more feedback on these few chapters, though."

In my experience, writing workshops worked best when the writer was still in process with their piece. Anytime a writer came into a workshop of mine with a fully finished story, the group's advice did little to change the writer's choices or perspective, and instead served to wound their ego. I had learned this firsthand the day before, in my first workshop of the Santa Barbara Writers Conference. A man debuted the first chapter of a novel he'd been working on about a time traveler who investigated the death of JFK. The group's advice to change the concept entirely did not land well.

The man began to read.

"So this is from, uh, chapter five:

Growing up in Tennessee, my mother and I lived alone with our maid, Betsy, as Papa left before I could walk or speak. Mama loved Betsy like she was one of our own. Betsy couldn't speak English very well, or read at all, but she was a mean cook.

She'd spend all day in the kitchen making the best meals

you'd ever taste. Then, after lunch, she'd pack up something for us for dinner and go home.

The only time we didn't see her was on the weekends, and I never knew what she did in that time.

One day, I asked Betsy why she couldn't read. I said:

'Well, Betsy, why don't you go take lessons down at the high school to learn how to read.'

Mama would have paid for her to go, too, because she loved Betsy so much. But Betsy said:

'Well what I need to do that for? Ain't gone change nothing no how.'"

The man drawled out a whiny, repugnant imitation of his childhood maid. My jaw dropped as a hot, angry flush spread over my face. I wanted to reach into my bag and text someone, but I couldn't.

"Well, one day, when I was around ten, Betsy stopped showing up for work. Two days went by and we didn't hear from her. One morning, Mama put me in the back of the convertible with some chicken soup and we drove out to a strange neighborhood. All the houses were small and looked badly put together. The dark men sitting on their porches watched us as we went by.

When Mama parked in front of one of the houses she told me to stay in the car. She said,

'This is where Betsy lives. I'm gonna go get her.'

I watched Mama walk up with the tin of soup and knock on the door. Two big Black men answered, their arms crossed. I couldn't hear what they were saying, but I could tell they wouldn't let Mama in to see Betsy. I couldn't see why they wouldn't let her in. She just wanted to help Betsy."

The faces of everyone else in the room screwed up in confusion or discomfort, but no one said a thing. I kept my gaze carefully focused on the carpet. It was orange. The circular pattern under my foot spread across the room, swirling beneath each of our shoes and disappearing beneath the darkness of the couches.

"The men told my Mama that Betsy was sick, and she'd come in later that week. When Mama got back to the car I asked her who those big scary men were and why we couldn't go see Betsy.

'Because they don't trust us,' Mama said.

'But why?' I asked her. 'Betsy's like family.'

'Well,' my Mama said. 'It's because we're white folks, and we don't belong here in the Black neighborhood.'

It was the first time that I realized someone could be treated differently by the color of their skin."

The man paused after this line, placing the printed manuscript down on his lap. He turned to me. His breath smelled of stale coffee; sharp and pungent. He was too close for me to not look him in the eye as he placed his hand on my bare knee.

"I'm so glad you're here for this part," he said.

A hot wave of anger and nausea rushed over me.

As the man picked up his manuscript to begin reading again, Lorelai finally spoke.

"–I'm so sorry, but I'm gonna have to stop you there because that made me very uncomfortable," she said. "Show of hands, who else here felt uncomfortable by that reading?"

In unison, we lifted our hands around the room. One woman threw me a pitying look.

"Uncomfortable?" the man said slowly. "No, no. I think you're misunderstanding. The story was about, uh, accepting differences, you know? I mean, we loved Betsy!"

He pulled a crooked smile, his eyes begging the others to understand. The man turned and looked at me.

"I think you're misunderstanding," he said.

I thought of the woman in the story and easily she could have been my grandmother; hadn't Grandma spent much of her life nannying white people like him? Didn't he know that hearing him talk that way made me want to spit? How could he have known?

And for him to touch me the way that he did–

Do not cry, I told myself. *You will not cry.*

"Here, maybe if I just keep reading–"

"No, no," said Lorelai, raising her hand. "I think that's enough."

A quiet settled over the room. The instructor cleared her throat, rubbing her hands together.

"How about we give the readings a break and try a writing exercise, huh? Is everyone okay with that?"

Marliee pressed her bony hands against her flowery dress and stood, turning to the table behind her. She inserted a CD into the old player on the table and pressed play. From it spilled a low, humming tone like a singing bowl. She breathed in deeply through her nose, letting her lids flutter shut.

"Close your eyes," said Lorelai. "We're going to try something."

She had a very soft voice, lilted, like a lullaby.

"Imagine," she said, "that you're lying in a beautiful meadow. It's stretched out and thick in silky grass. There's the scent of wildflowers, and the sound of birds. The earth is warm and comforting.

Imagine a magical train, in a world that's still and safe. In a world where all the scary feelings would just slip away. In this place, only good things will happen. In this place, you'll never feel alone.

Imagine a train. It will go where you want it to go and do only what you want it to do. You can hear it coming from far in the distance. It comes closer and closer.

Choose where you want to sit. The choice is yours. Let the train go wherever you want it to go."

I closed my eyes. My whole body was tense; bubbling and hot inside, yet cold from the breeze. It seemed stupid, this little prompt. But I decided to try.

In my head, I stood on the platform of the Amtrak train station in Goleta. My bags were heavy in my arms as the train opened in front of me and I remembered the last time I visited Eli.

I took my usual seat, on the second story, behind the stairs on the right hand side; that would be the side that faced the ocean as we traveled up the coast towards San Jose.

My train was a busy one, full of chatter. I envisioned the other travelers: the newlywed Santa Barbara vacationers, the elderly woman watching the sea, the other sleepy students heading home. As my body jolted up the coast, I leaned my head against the bumpy window and watched the world go by.

I thought I knew where my train was going. I thought of the long train rides up north, ones where I stepped on in the afternoon and got off when the night turned dark. I felt anticipation, the expectation of someone who loved me waiting at the last stop.

But it never came. Instead I saw the cityscape of Los Angeles passing me by, a heat rising around me.

Then, I was back in Long Beach, standing in my teenage bedroom. It was exactly as I left it when I moved for college. My drawers were stuffed with old textbooks and journals and empty vape pens. The closet was full of dirty laundry I never bothered to wash. At one point, I suppose I thought it would all just disappear while I was gone; be thrown out or cleaned. But there it all was.

I laid down on the set of white and pink floral sheets that I had not washed since September, in a bed that no longer felt quite like mine.

"Open your eyes," said Lorelai.

My eyes fluttered open. I had almost forgotten where I was. The low humming music still played in the background, and Lorelai sat with her hands folded on her lap, watching me intently. She looked around the room at each of us.

"Now," she said softly, "take out a piece of paper and write. Write about where you went on your journey, and what you saw. What you felt. I once was able to write a whole book using this exercise, just starting with the idea of a train."

Lorelai reached behind her and pressed pause on the stereo. Only the sound of the wind against the curtains remained.

Across from me, the boy with the curly hair was already writing, fingers dancing across the keyboard of his laptop, while the woman sitting next to him dug around in her purse for a pen, then sat hesitantly with it poised over a notebook. The older man sitting next to me simply sat, staring at his hands.

I reached into my bag for a pen. I hadn't expected to write much that day, so all I brought with me was my laptop and a diary. It was a small journal with an ornate blue cover that I had hardly used since I bought it, though I had intended to begin journaling again after the breakup. I opened the little book and pressed my pen to its page.

"Who would like to start?" Lorelai asked once the scribbling stopped. Everyone stared at each other from across the room, an air of uncertainty around us.

I raised my hand next, less sure of myself than I'd been in any workshop before. Still, I felt like I *had* to read. It was the same feeling I'd had in Harvey's workshop during my first year in Santa Barbara.

Marliee smiled softly and gestured for me to begin.

"The train goes both ways," I began, looking up tentatively at the group. "Up and down the California coast, encrusted in mansions and craggly cliff sides, crumbled like cobbler. I sleep-walk down cabins in LA underbellies of graffitied concrete and ducks swimming in sewage lakes, yet sweaty heat feels like.. home."

My voice cracked, the word coming out in two distinct halves. The people in the room watched me, heavy and wide-eyed.

"Feels like dad's busted Toyota driving towards Compton

without the air con, and the communal piano being played at Union station. In LA it's always day, always sunny. But, all roads lead back to San Jose.

When I arrive up North it's dark. Little Diridon station, the man who smells of pee sleeping at the bus stop. A small girl with long, dressed in all gray stands waiting. Dark as this city. Warm as home. The train goes both ways."

Vulnerability—true blatant honesty of it—was the part of writing nonfiction I'd always struggled with. In real life, I was often emotionally closed off to the people around me. As I read what I'd written to the group of strangers around me, I felt something like a dam break. I began to cry so heavily I could barely get the words out.

What did any of them know of this train, I thought, or of home, or of the girl I'd just lost. I wondered if this place would ever truly be home to me. I desperately wanted it to be. I wanted to feel at home in my life and in my choices and in myself. I wanted it so badly it hurt.

"Thank you," Lorelai said and patted my shoulder. The other writers looked at me with soft, sorry eyes. I sat there in the cold sweat of it all, and halfway through the next person's reading, excused myself from the room. I called an early Uber home, alone.

That was the last day that I attended the Conference.

I decided that I did not need this conference of people to

validate me to be a writer. To be a real writer I needed to know who I was.

When I returned home from the conference, Isla Vista looked starkly different than it had before. It was the time of year in a college town when everything emptied. In the growing heat of July, the streets of Isla Vista, usually lined block to block with cars, were vacant as the student body migrated for the season. Construction crews filled the empty apartment buildings, painting over the chipped walls and filling in holes with plaster.

The living room of my apartment, once filled to the brim with my roommate's storage bins and old furniture, stood empty and quiet. Like me, its emptiness held endless possibilities.

Yet, as every friend and every coworker made their plans for the summer, discussing family trips and all the people they were excited to see, I felt myself drawn to home.

Two weeks after the conference, I stood on the busy platform of Goleta station. I stared across the tracks at orange poppies blooming on the edge of the 101 freeway, the cars rushing by as my train screeched to a halt before me. The platform was full of students toting oversized duffel bags and suitcases, awaiting home.

"..Amtrak is not liable for any loss of personal property, so please keep an eye on your belongings and report any suspicious behavior for the safety of other passengers," the crackly-voiced woman said over the loudspeakers for the third time that day.

Behind me, a girl tapped the shoulder of the boy standing next to her.

"Do you know if this is the train to San Diego?" she asked.

The boy pulled his headphones off of his left ear.

"Uh, I think so?" he said. "I only go as far as Ventura."

"First stop at Goleta station!" someone yelled from a farther car as the train doors slid open. "Now boarding, first stop!"

I grabbed my carry-on, a 30-pound pink duffel bag, and threw my overweight backpack and tote bag on my shoulder and boarded.

The Pacific Coastliner, the train that I took to Los Angeles, began its trip in Goleta and hugged the coastline from Santa Barbara to Ventura for a five hour trip. In Santa Barbara we skated past a kingdom of white Spanish colonial-style castles. At Santa Barbara station, all the families out to picnic at a park nearby waved at our passing train. By the swingset, a mother stood with three toddlers, all linked by hand, instructing them to "say hi!"

I lifted my hand and waved back, though they could not see me. Then, as the train tracks brought us into the backyards of beachside homes, I peeked into their decadent gardens, imagining swimming in their pools and picking fruit from the trees.

Somewhere past Carpeneria, the path to the ocean cleared and I could see straight over the rocky cliffside to the waves crashing frothy white onto them. As the rocks drew back farther and farther, my view was nothing but golden sand, the wide angle of the 101 curving like a bow in front of us into Ventura. Somewhere on that freeway, now far behind us, was the lane where Eli crashed her car. In another life, I would see its skeleton, fuming smoke as a tow truck pulled it away. Now, all I could see was blue.

Between Ventura and Los Angeles I let the soft, chugging rhythm of the train lull me asleep. I did not wake until a man's suitcase bumped my seat and a bright green bus stop outside my window announced in big white letters: City of Glendale.

A line of people shuffled through the train's walkway towards the stairs in front of me as the doors below opened to Glendale. On the platform, a young girl ran into the arms of an older man, a little boy beside them holding a stuffed animal tightly between his arms. I rubbed my fingers over my dry eyes and opened my phone.

Text me when you're close, my father said.

The train traced the track alongside the L.A. river, a family of ducks swimming across the surface. Red and white graffiti patchworked the concrete channel, the colors bright against the gray sky as the afternoon burnt away.

I'm close.

"Welcome to Los Angeles, next stop is Union Station. If you are getting off at Union station, please gather your things and make your way to the bottom of the train. We will be making a short fifteen minute stop in Los Angeles for the dining cart to reload and then be taking off at 6:15, so don't leave your seat if you're continuing on. Once again, that's Union Station. Arriving at Union Station."

The Surfliner always landed at terminal eight or nine, a long walk from the lobby of Union Station. The heat of Los Angeles hit me immediately as I stepped down from the train onto the crowded platform. The other L.A. riders shifted their luggage in their hands, anxious to board as I dragged my duffel down the ramp and into the station. Breathlessly, I shuffled through a long passageway to the lobby. The lights bounced brightly off the brown tiled floor, while boarding times blinked at me in green LEDs from above.

People bustled up and down the hall, some with small backpacks heading for a Metro, others, like me, overwhelmed with suitcases and carry-ons. Amtrak only allowed two carry-ons per ride, but I always snuck in an extra purse or tote bag to take things back with. My tote slipped from my shoulder as a golf cart rattled past me, toting an older couple and their monogrammed luggage.

At the edge of the hall, a dreadhead man leant against a mural of Leimert park humming along to the sound of the lobby's piano. Chandeliers hung in parallel lines over the lobby from the beamed ceiling, dragging one's eyes towards the yellow arch of the station's entrance. The fading summer light shone through tall windows alongside them. To my left, the long lines for Wetzel's Pretzels and Starbucks mingled together.

"Are you here?" I shouted into my phone over the excitement of the lobby and the honking cars on my sister's side of the phone. I passed under the yellow arch, hands full and arms aching as I rushed towards an open door.

"We're pulling up to the pick-up spot, it's just taking forever," Margot said. "Why is it so busy today?"

"I don't know," I heaved. I tried to make it through the door before it swung closed. "I guess everyone's heading home."

My father's gray Toyota drove past the entrance, curving into the far right lane labeled: "Pick-up zone. Do not stop." I pushed through those few last steps towards him and let the weight finally drop from my body. My dad swung open the driver's side door.

"Hi Daddy!" I smiled.

"Hey love," he grabbed me from the back of the head, pulling me toward him. I threw my arms around him as he leaned down to kiss my forehead. He didn't say much, but he held me longer than usual.

"Mayaaa," Margot squealed, hopping out of the passenger seat. My sister was three years older than me and two inches shorter.

Her plump face was screwed up in a childish grin as I buried myself in her hug.

"You have too much stuff," my dad groaned, lifting up my pink duffel to load into his trunk.

My sister and I held each other by our forearms, taking the sight of the other in.

"Your hair is different," she said, deadpan.

"It always is. Why are you wearing crocs?" I asked.

She tugged at the t-shirt branding her job's logo and rolled her eyes. "I just got off work."

"Let's go," my dad said, slamming the trunk shut, "before traffic gets worse."

In the car, I threw off my sweatshirt and let my sister's chatter of work and school wash over me. She told me about the raccoon in the backyard that had been scaring our cat and my mom's incessant worrying about whether or not it would give our cat rabies. Across the street from Union Station, I could see the restaurant off Olvera street where our Uncle Paul had taken us for lunch a few years ago, remembering my first time at the Station.

"And how's Grandpa?" I asked. My dad's father had been taken to the hospital at the beginning of summer after breaking his hip. During his exam, they found cancer. No one knew how serious it was yet or how long his stay would be. At 85, the body healed much slower than it did earlier in life. The uncertainty of it eerily reminded of how we all felt about Uncle Paul.

"He's doing good. Your aunt got him into a different hospital, the other one wasn't getting him the right treatment," my dad said soberly. "But he's doing fine. Don't worry about it, sweetheart."

Unlike last time, when I didn't truly know how ill my uncle was until my dad called to tell me he had passed, I wanted to stay constantly updated about my grandparents. I did worry, but I knew that to my father worrying would do no good. So, I didn't push any further.

"So," I said, changing the subject. "Auntie Alice is really not hosting a party for Fourth of July this year?"

Margot swiftly turned around in her seat to face me. "Nope! It's 'cause her and Uncle Mike are going to visit Kerynn in Oregon," she said, smacking her gums. "Fourth of July is so weird when we can't celebrate with a big party!"

After 45 minutes on the freeway, we exited the 91 to Long Beach. The dispensary on the corner of the exit announced: "NEW! LEGAL CANNABIS 21+", despite it having been open for over three years. Across the street, in the auto repair shop parking lot, a taco truck with a scrolling LED sign read: "Tacos, Taquitos, Tortas!" A single customer lingered outside the truck.

"You know, I never see a line at this place," my dad said, as he always did when we passed it. "They can't be any good if there's no line."

"They have to be okay if they're always open," I said. "Why don't you just try it?"

"Nah," he said, shaking his head. "Can't be any good."

On a row of slanted houses, my parent's white and yellow house in Long Beach was marked by the tall palm tree that sprouted below my bedroom window. My sister and I's bedroom windows looked out to the street like two big eyes on the house's face, shrouded behind a set of lopsided palms that my dad had strapped to a pole of wood. From there the lawn sloped down towards the street, a thin walkway leading from the driveway to a small white porch.

My mother's black Honda sat on the incline of the driveway while my sister's baby blue sedan sat on the side of the street, below the tree that sprayed sap. My dad parked behind her on the street, as he always did, and the family cat ran from across the street, perching at the front door for us.

"Hi lovie!" my mother said, greeting me at the door. She was dressed in her work clothes: a red t-shirt that read "Teacher's are worth it!" with jeans and a pair of sneakers. I leaned down and laid my head against her shoulder while I hugged her, as if I was still a child. She smelled like the new leave-in conditioner she was using that day; passion-fruit and honey.

The wind rustled the trees outside and she jumped.

"Ooh!" she cried. "Was that that damn raccoon?"

My sister dropped her body onto the couch behind her.

"No, that's not the raccoon," Margot said, rolling her eyes into her head.

My mom ignored her and gripped my arms. "Did Margot tell you about the raccoon? Nasty thing's been scaring Nibs!"

The family cat had not moved from where he sat in the doorway, licking his privates. My mother told me he was sure to get rabies being outside all the time.

"He's been sleeping in your room again," my sister teased.

"It better not be a mess in there," I told her.

"Don't blame me, blame your father," said my mother.

It was a mess. Along with all the crap I left behind when I went to college—an over-filled bookcase, a dresser full of old pajamas and jeans and textbooks, unused hair products and unwashed clothes filling up the closet—my family took the liberty of filling my bedroom with all the crap they no longer wanted as well. In the space between my bed and my dresser, my dad had left a collection of indigenous artwork he'd been collecting from garage sales and swap meets. Next to it, there was a garbage bag of goodwill donations from my sister, and two unworn boxes of shoes from my mom.

I found space to drop down my bags and fell back onto the

bed. The sheets had not been cleaned since the last time I'd been there, three months ago. They were covered in crumbs of dirt and cat hair. But it was mine. Possibly the only space in the world that was truly mine.

At the end of the day, that childhood bedroom was where I would have to come and rest my head. If I did not clean the room, no one would.

The day of the Fourth, my dad pulled out the old grill he used twice a year and lit it up. He bought two packs of chicken thighs, one pack of chicken breast, and a pack of pre seasoned carne asada to throw on. The meat sat, either thawing or already cooked, in large tupperware containers that took up space on our kitchen counters. My sister pulled hot links and grilled corn out of the fridge for him to add on while I cut fruit salad and mixed potato salad.

My favorite Fourth of Julys were big celebrations held at my Aunt's house in Inglewood. Members of the extended family would gather there for a big cookout that led up to the neighborhood's competing firework displays. It was better than the firework shows at Disneyland. From far away, I found fireworks boring. But, up close, the pop of them overhead felt electrifying. My dad thought it was just a competition of who could waste the most money, so we didn't buy any fireworks when it was just us. At half past 10, I could hear the sky cracking farther out in the neighborhood.

"Do you want to go for a walk?" I asked Margot as she handed me a can of Cutwater. It was my first of the night while she and my mother were both on their second.

Outside the back door, my mom and dad were puttering around in the backyard as the grill blew up big clouds of gray smoke. They tasted fruit from the five different tomato plants my dad had added to his vegetable garden that year while the blue sparks glowed above them.

"Sure, where?" Margot asked.

I told my sister, "The park."

I meant Heartwell park, which was down the street from our house and a few blocks from our old high school, but it didn't need to be said. It was just the Park, where everyone at our school would hang out after 3 p.m., where I'd meet my best friend in the mornings to walk to class, where I'd gotten high for the first time in one of the bathrooms.

My sister and I left our parents to the garden and slipped out of the house in large hoodies and slippers. At the back of the park, there was a small, fenced-in playground meant for younger kids. We climbed over the locked gate and saddled ourselves on the swings as fireworks filled the sky above, loud as gunshots. Already fuzzy and warm from the alcohol, I sparked the joint I'd smuggled in my backpack and offered my sister a hit.

"No thanks," Margot said, squinting at me with curiosity.

I held the joint to my lips and pulled, coughing on the smoke.

"What, you don't smoke anymore?" I asked her.

"No, not really. It makes me feel weird," she said. Margot twisted herself in her swing, the chains wrapping around her body before spinning her back in the other direction.

It was pitch black out beyond the reach of the streetlights. Perhaps we should have felt a bit on guard, but it was hard to feel unsafe in a place so familiar.

I didn't get to see my sister often. From when I was just starting high school–the year she left home for college–to the time that I graduated college, we had not spent more than a year and a half living in the same place at the same time. It wasn't until we were stuck in a house together during the Pandemic that I realized just how much I missed having a sister; someone who understood and reflected me in every way, even when we seemed so different. Looking at her now was like looking in a funhouse mirror, our bodies and temperaments slightly altered by the years spent apart.

I stubbed the joint in the sand and threw the butt away.

"Guess you can't really smoke at home anyway," I said. "Hey, did I ever tell you about the writer's conference thing?"

"What, that thing you went to?" Margot asked, raising an eyebrow. "Did something happen?"

I smiled impishly, "Well, first, this weird lady comes up and slips me a note telling me she's 'looking for a Black writer for a project,' and she doesn't even speak to me."

Margot snorted, "Okay, weird."

"And then, my old professor basically asked to sleep with me!"

She stopped spinning in her swing. "Maya, what?"

"Okay, well not really," I said quickly. "He asked to sleep in my hotel room, but that's how I interpreted it."

Margot looked caught between concern and hilarity, same as I had been. "Maya, that's really bad!" She brought her hands to her face and peeked at me between her fingers.

"No, no it's fine!" I laughed. "Nothing happened, everyone's just so weird there–like, oh! There was this weird old guy who read a story about his Black maid growing up."

I widened my eyes. "In Tennessee, Margot. His Black maid."

"Are you even learning anything up there?" Margot asked, shaking her head.

I shrugged. "I think so?"

I leaned back and balanced my body on the swing, staring up at the blinking sky. It was a blurry sight, my head going fuzzy.

"So, how's the whole girlfriend thing?" said Margot. I couldn't see the expression on her face when she said it.

"Oh, we broke up. I broke up with her," I corrected.

Margot was one of the only people that piece of information came out easily to. I felt a pang of sadness in my chest, thinking about it again. But the feeling lessened each time I remembered her. From a distance, the relationship looked endlessly complicated, and being without out did not feel like such a loss.

"Oh," said Margot.

"Yeah." I let my body go limp, head and legs hanging off of the swing.

"Sorry," Margot said, though she didn't need to be. I sat up and looked her in the eyes. She looked truly sorry. I smiled, trying to show her it was okay.

"It's cool. I'm glad it happened, I think."

"Hmph," she said, neither agreeing or disagreeing.

Behind us, a bush made a rustling sound and I jumped instinctively.

"Oh my god, you think that's the raccoon?"

"Don't start!" Margot cried and we both burst into laughter.

"I'm sorry, I'm sorry–"

"She's been acting so crazy about it!"

"I know!" I said.

"You know, I can't even leave the house without Mommy

asking where I'm going?" Margot's eyes widened as she leaned in and spoke in exaggerated tones.

"She wants to know where I am *all the time*; where I'm going, when I'll be back. She'll even call me at work: 'Where are you?'

Look, the other day she called me at 10 a.m., and said 'You're not home, where are you?' and I said, 'I'm at the gym,' because I was at the gym! She said 'Oh, okay. Can you pick me something up from the store?'"

Margot threw her arms out in exasperation.

"I can't take it!" she said.

"Yeah, see, that's why I can't be living here!" I snickered. "God, why don't you just move?"

"What and start paying rent?" Margot scoffed. "Hell no, I like having money."

"At what cost?"

Margot sucked at her teeth and shrugged. "I've got one more year until I finish my teaching credential. I just want to get through the rest of school without having to think about money."

A series of blue and green fireworks shot up from a house down the street and we gasped. It was the time of the night when the neighbors set up big mortar shell fireworks in their backyards, blowing hundreds of dollars up in the sky.

"Do you think we'll ever live together again," I asked out of nowhere.

Margot turned to me, her expression wide and earnest. "I don't know."

"Well," I said. "I hope so. I miss you."

Margot smiled. "I miss you too."

The fireworks at the Park were nothing compared to the displays in Inglewood, but they felt magnificent.

When we arrived back at the house an hour later, it was nearly midnight. I found my mother sitting on the couch in her nightshirt and bonnet, two drinks deep, cackling at the TV. On the couch she'd spread a large blanket underneath her while the cat sat by her feet.

"Margot, Margot–" my mom said, almost breathless from her own laughter. "You have to see this, come here!"

On the television, the von Trapp siblings ascended the stairs of their parent's mansion, singing their goodbyes to their party guests. Dressed in small gray shorts and matching knee socks, the youngest brother sang his goodbye in a girlish high pitch that always made my mother giggle.

"Goodbyeee," my mother crooned, her cheeks ruddy.

"Oh no," my sister side-eyed me and pressed her fingers to her forehead. "Not this."

My mother loved old musicals like *Grease*, *West Side Story*, and *The Sound of Music* because she'd done dance while she was in high school. She maintained a love for anything theatrical and liked to punish us with it, making us watch the films over and over again.

"Find a new movie!" my father shouted through the window from the backyard. He had been listening to her sing for the past hour.

"I need another drink," Margot said.

"Whaaa," my mother slurred and held out her hand. "Maya come here."

My favorite von Trapp farewell was the littlest daughter, Gretl's. She wore a white babydoll dress and clean white tights as she lifted herself up the staircase, step by step, before laying to sleep at the top one.

"Goodnight.." her siblings sang, lifting her sleeping body.

"Goodnight.." my mother sang along.

I shook my head, but sang back to the final note. "Goodnight."

"Put on the Wiz!" Margot shouted from the kitchen.

"Ooh, that's a good one!" my mother dropped my hand and scrambled for the remote.

For the next two hours we sang along to the Wiz getting drunker and drunker and giddier and giddier. As he liked to, my dad stopped into the house intermittently to use the bathroom and make fun of us.

"Come on, how many times have you seen this?" he asked my mom as she geared up for Dorothy to meet her Glinda, the Good Witch.

"Shush!" my mom said. "This is the good part."

Like the *Sound of Music*, I never fully understood *The Wiz* when I watched it as a child. Mentions of Nazis and minstrelsy went right over my head. Back then, I was simply mesmerized by the glittering costumes and joyful dancing.

To those who'd never seen it, I described my favorite movie as "the Black Wizard of Oz". It was a beautiful explosion of motown and technicolor. Instead of beginning in Kansas, Diana Ross' Dorothy got swept away in a snowstorm in Harlem and transported to a gritty, apocalyptic New York cityscape. Her version of Oz mirrored themes of urban gentrification and Black reclamation as Diana Ross' Dorothy and Michael Jackson's Scarecrow searched for home in a place that was no longer theirs. All of their references to home looked a lot like mine; soulful singing and big family dinners.

All throughout college, I found myself drawn to the movie again, playing the soundtrack on repeat because it really did feel like home to me. But, when I tried to play it for my roommates, or my partner, the feeling didn't stick.

Beside me, just as Lena Horne's Glinda told Dorothy to

"Think of home," my mother prepared to sing. Diana Ross looked up at the camera, mournfully, dressed in her iconic fro and ruffled purple blouse.

"Home?" said Diana, her glassy eyes sparkling. My mother took a deep breath to follow her.

"Home?" She turned and took my sister's face in her hand.

"You're late, you lush," Margot said and pushed her away, but my mother kept singing.

My mom's voice quavered as she rose from the couch, arms spread like wings.

"I have had my mind spun around in space, and yet I've watching gro-o-owing," she sang into my sister's face, reaching a hand out to me.

"I'm out," my dad snorted.

I giggled, but grabbed her hand and she sang. I sang along, feeling light and warm and fuzzy.

"If you're listening, God, please–don't make it hard to know if we should believe the things that we see.

Tell us, should we run away? Should we try and stay? Or would it better just to let things be?

Living here, in this brand new world might be a fantasy,

But it taught me to love,

So it's *real*. Real to me.

And I've learned that we must look inside our hearts to find—

A world full of love,

Like yours, like mine,

Like home."

That past year, more than ever, I had felt what it was to truly be alone. I no longer wanted to close my family out of my life. They were all that I had.

How long had it taken me to realize that things were different now, and that this was actually where I wanted to be?

The next day I began to clean out my closet.

Namesake

I knew when I began to write this book that my grandmother would not be alive by the time I finished. I wondered what it would mean to bear her name while she was not on this Earth. I found it impossible to imagine life without her.

Each time that I visited home throughout college, Grandma Ruby seemed to grow more and more frail. The gaps of months between my visits made the changes between each of us more drastic. She'd marvel at how I was growing, my more childish features like my chubby cheeks and puffy eyes thinning away. Each step that I took towards independence was a step away from home. In the meantime, Grandma was able to do less around the house on her own.

As Grandma got older, I learned how much I needed to care for those around me, not just for their sake but for my own. I did not know how to show love if not through service. I needed to take care of the dishes in my grandma's sink after Sunday dinners so that she would not have to. I needed to bring her floss and tissues so she did not have to stand up and get them herself. It made me feel gratified.

Maybe this was because Grandma Ruby had always needed someone, or something, to care for. Caring for other things and people seemed to fulfill Grandma. She loved tending to her plants and caring for animals. If you so much as needed a napkin in her house, she would get up from where she was sitting in the other room and walk to the kitchen to get it for you.

I liked to think Grandma and I were just alike because I shared her name: Maya Rubylee Johnson. I think that at times, she thought so too. As a teenager, she'd pull out old photos from her jewelry box and say things like:

"You do your hair just like I did."

One photo showed her in a braided updo that wrapped around her head exactly as I had my hair styled that day. The funny thing about it was that she said it as if I had copied *her*, without even knowing. I felt some strange cosmic tension between us, me replicating her decades later. She was always like a prophet to me, or a witch.

My grandmother spent much of her time puttering around her apartment for one. She wore great red and green and purple robes and turbans and created magic in giant pots, singing haunting songs of God from memory. I wanted her joy for life.

I wished she could have always stayed that joyful and vibrant. The last time that I visited my grandmother in her apartment, at the beginning of last summer, she was wearing a red and black patterned scarf around her head and watching Russian films on Youtube. She didn't seem very off, at first. She was a bit tired, but energetic enough to talk about the Russian culture and politics she had learned through days of watching those films. We had lunch at her apartment, just the two of us, while my parents took care of business at my Grandpa's apartment.

Halfway through the movie, her teeth started chattering intermittently.

"Are you okay, grandma?" I asked.

She smiled and waved me off, snuggling deeper into her favorite reclining chair.

"Oh, I'm alright, baby. I just had a bit of a stomach bug this morning." Grandma coughed into her arm and reached for a water bottle on her coffee table. I quickly put it into her hand. Her eyes looked dull, suddenly.

"Thank you, baby," she smiled, the soft wrinkles of her face joining together.

In a few minutes, she asked me:

"Baby, could you go and get me some aspirin from the

bathroom? It's behind the mirror, I think I still have a little headache."

"Of course, Grandma," I said. I wanted to do anything I could to help her, but without my parents and without a car I felt worried. In the bathroom I texted my dad:

You need to come back. I think something's wrong with Grandma.

When Grandma's shakes did not stop, she asked that I bring her a blanket. And when that did not help, a heating pad. Grandma continued to cough and to shake, though she insisted that her symptoms were just that of a cold or something along those lines. Her skin faded to a pale gray and I got a familiar dread in the pit of my stomach. I felt like she could slip away at any second.

More than anything, death brought up feelings of regret for me. While I was away at college, I regretted not being home as much as I could have, for my uncle and for my grandmother.

After the Thanksgiving that I brought Eli home to meet my family, my grandma and I had a bit of a drift. I spent much of the time that I could have spent with my family worrying about my relationship. After we'd broken up and Grandma fell ill, this guilt made a wreck out of me.

In my mind, part of the problem was that my grandmother had trouble acknowledging my sexuality. I told myself that I would not deny myself for her, or for anyone else, because I felt, intrinsically, a sense of disapproval and judgment from my family around those topics. I projected it. But, the truth was that my grandmother did not grow up in a world where my life choices were possible. I was asking for complete understanding over a situation even I could not fully comprehend. Her acceptance should have been enough.

But I wanted to shove it in her face, make her swallow me whole.

"Grandma's upset that I am not spending Christmas at home," I told my mom on the phone sometime after Thanksgiving. "She's upset I'm spending it with Eli. She thinks I should be home."

The year before, I'd spent Christmas Eve in my grandma's apartment. During the holidays, she filled her space with festive figurines and red and green tchotchkes, all of her Christmas cards out for display. She was the one I most associated that holiday with, as my parents weren't big on celebrating it. It was a special memory that seemed to hurt my grandmother when I told her I planned to spend the holidays with my girlfriend's family that year.

"No one's gonna live your life but you," my mom sighed. "You know she loves you, why are you letting this become a thing?"

Why hadn't I fully accepted myself on my own yet? Grandma was not afraid to tell me what she thought I should have been doing, even if she still did not fully acknowledge that Eli existed. When

I brought my relationship up on the phone the other line would go silent. Then, after a while, Grandma would topic would change entirely, and she once again wouldn't understand why I wouldn't be home for Christmas.

"Just let her be who she'll be," said my mother. "You don't need her to understand every aspect of your life."

"But I want her to," I cried childishly. "I want to have real adult relationships with the people around me, not ones where I have to hide who I am."

"You can have adult relationships without needing someone to see all of you. Your grandparents aren't going to be alive forever, you know. You don't want to have any regrets once they're gone."

My mother's father had passed away when I was 10, and she'd lost her younger brother before then. When Grandad was sick she made sure she didn't regret a single thing, she told me. No matter what difference she and Grandad had, by the end of his life she had no regrets.

I thought of my grandma and I the evening of last Thanksgiving, sitting on fold up chairs in my backyard while the rest of the family cleaned up from dessert. She'd asked me out there with her, wanting a moment alone. The orange of the sun passed over her soft, creped skin and she spoke to me softly.

"You know I'll always love you," she'd said, though confusion clouded her eyes. I wish I'd truly understood then just how much it meant to have that.

My mom waited silently on the other end of the phone. I pressed my palm to my eyes and held back tears.

"I know."

A year later, after I'd visited my grandma and she fell ill, my parents took Grandma Ruby to the hospital. There was a sickness in her gut, and no one knew how or why. Over the next few months, as Grandpa slowly recovered, Grandma was transferred from facility to facility as her doctors tried all kinds of different treatments to get her better.

Then, one day in early winter, my dad called me at work.

I was just getting started on a long closing shift. I didn't know how I knew to check my phone as it rang on silent, but I did. And as soon as I saw my dad's contact photo I knew.

"Hey love, what are you up to?"

He was sniffling, his voice strained. My dad didn't cry often, most men don't. I knew this routine.

"I'm at work," I told him tentatively.

It was half past ten p.m. on a Saturday and I knew he was going to tell me to call him back later; to put work and school and my life in Isla Vista first, and worry about them later.

My dad began: "Okay, call me when you get off-"

"No," I cut him off. "Tell me now."

Already, I had excused myself through the back entrance of the restaurant, standing in the dark, lonely parking lot I left through each night alone, next to the dirty mats and trash cans. Grandma hadn't passed, he told me, but her condition was only worsening. Without a thought, I called out of my shift early and left town the next day. All I knew was that I had to see her.

When I arrived at the hospital, there was no need to voice what was coming next. It was obvious in the way my mother gently wiped the spit from Grandma's mouth, or the extra time my dad held me to him, just happy that I was there.

The hospital room was drafty and my sister shivered in the corner. I wrapped my arms around her and leaned her head against my chest, as if I was the bigger sister. Sometimes I did feel as if I had to be bigger. I wanted to fix things, hold it all together.

"Maya, is that you?" Grandma was only half-conscious, extremely drowsy from her meds and struggling to keep her eyes open. "Why aren't you school?" she mumbled.

I grabbed her hand from her side and held it in mine.

"Because I wanted to see you, of course," I said.

Her eyes fluttered open and she smiled.

"Hi, baby."

"Hi, Grandma," I said.

She was very thirsty those days, so we bought her packs of water bottles and pre-opened them so that she could drink without help from the hospital staff. Grandma asked me to rearrange her things for her and help her find her flossers so she could clean her teeth. Then, I helped her moisturize her feet, taking off her socks and rubbing lotion into the dry skin of her soles before putting them back on.

"Oh, and can you fix the blanket under my feet," Grandma said. "I just like it a certain way, keeps them elevated."

I leaned over and kissed her cheek. "Anything for you, Grandma."

I knew I was losing her. I wanted to do anything I could to make up for lost time.

When Grandma finally did pass, I tried my best not to cry. Her funeral was held at the family church, same as Uncle Paul's.

My grandmother's immediate family—my aunts and uncles and cousins and I—all stood at the church's entrance, waiting for us to enter in the procession. I hadn't spoken all day. I was coming home for the funeral because I had to, because I would hate myself if I didn't, and then I could go back to IV and pretend it all didn't exist. But as I looked around at them all, I felt the tears coming, unable to hold it in any longer.

Around the side of the church, I saw my dad walking towards the back entrance. For some reason, he was against the idea of a procession. I slipped away from my mother and sister and followed him, nearly tripping in my chunky heels.

"Daddy!" I called out.

He stopped at the door to the church's kitchen and turned to me. I tried to smile, my eyes watering as I walked to him. My voice broke.

"I can't do this," I said.

My dad held me in his arms, my head pressed into his chest. I also had not seen him cry yet, either.

"It's okay," he sniffed. "We'll do this together."

I did not tell him about the regret or how my mother had been right. I wanted to tell him, someone, that I was sorry; that I didn't know if I had done enough and I or fully made things right. I couldn't get that time back, she was gone.

Instead, when my uncle invited those in attendance to speak in her honor, I stood.

I did not speak at Uncle Paul's funeral, out of fear that I'd say the wrong thing, and I regretted it for months after. So, for weeks leading up to Grandma's funeral, no matter how I didn't want to, I wrote a speech for Grandma Ruby. And I read it again and again and again, until I could recite it in my head, until I knew just what to say:

"Growing up, Grandma Ruby was my favorite person. She was always kind of magical, knew how to do everything and cook anything. She is to me what a woman should be, kind, giving, generous. I wanted to be just like her. Everything I do, I do for her."

I couldn't make up for the past. I just wanted to set her memory right.

When I got back to school, all I thought of was my grandmother. In the days after the funeral, I expected my father to be inconsolable; to fall into some deep depression that he would never rise out of. But, like it did for my mother, and like it would for me, life had to go on. And we had each other.

As much as I was still sad, I forced myself not to ignore the grief inside of me. I wanted to keep thinking of my grandmother. I thought of her as I watered my plants, and as I cooked, and as I sang. I wanted to live for her, and I saw her in all the beauty around me.

I'm a strong believer that everything starts where it ends. My grandmother stood at the center of my family. She was the center of every meal, every celebration, every gossip campaign. As a child she looked nearly six feet tall, a scarf wrapped around her balding head like Sojourner Truth. And she was my namesake, which meant I wanted to be just like her.

In middle school, I interviewed my grandmother for a school family tree project. I'd lost the tapes long ago; they were much too valuable records to be kept by a twelve-year-old, and it was something I always regretted. In her apartment in Santa Monica, I propped my phone on a set of old blankets, looked her in the eyes, and let her tell me about her life for the first time.

Though I'd written her story a million ways a million different times, I still doubted myself when writing about her. My grandmother was the mother of a whole community. What right do I have to tell her story, and how many others would I contradict; who, what would I leave out.

How could I not know her fully, yet feel like her existence was all of me?

Accepting my grandmother was accepting all of me. Same as accepting my dad, my mom, and my ex-girlfriend. It was what I'd been asking everyone else around me to do. To see me with all of my complications and contradictions and to understand, after all that death and tragedy and rebirth that we had been through.

It was funny, I wondered if it was ever really my family that I had needed to accept me, or Santa Barbara and its community of writers, or if I really was the one who didn't fully accept me. It was only once I learned to accept my family as it was—perfectly imperfect, ever changing and growing, and not given each day—that I learned to accept myself.

There was so much I had taken for granted, because it was never "enough". I was never pretty enough, smart enough, Black enough, worthy enough for love and success. I needed to let myself simply be.

Through that middle school project, I learned that my grandmother grew up on a farm in Mississippi, back in time when an absolute stranger would come to the door looking for food it was expected for her mother but put him up for the whole night. My grandma left school around the fifth grade. At sixteen she ran away from home. There was peanut butter cake cooling in the kitchen and she had just got a whooping from her mother, so she decided it was time to leave. She borrowed a boat and went to stay with her Aunt in Arkansas, but ended up in California.

She had a love for British literature and old films. She loved to cook. She loved being a mother and a grandmother.

She was intensely religious, and knew the whole hymn book by heart. She believed the best way to be a Christian was through your actions; to live a life worthy of Christ. She would give you the clothes off her back if she felt you needed them more. And she could never truly hate anyone.

She wanted a writer in the family.

Acknowledgements

Thank you to all of those who helped me along in my journey as a writer here at UC Santa Barbara. Thank you first to my classmates and cohort in the College of Creative Studies, a strange and eclectic group of creatives who have been my backbone on campus, always able to provide emotional support and constructive critique. I am forever grateful for the community I have found, it has been an honor to support and be supported by you all in our respective journeys as emerging writers.

Thank you also to my professors at CCS, an integral part of the community we have created within this college. Thank you for expanding my understanding of what nonfiction can be and giving me the space to reimagine my experiences. Thank you to Ellen Whittet for her keen eye and editing prowess, without which I would not have the self-assurance to finish this book. Thank you to Anna Jay, Giulia Zappia, and Sonny Yiu, who all lent their time and creativity to the creation of this project. Thank you to Diana Raab and the Raab Writing Fellows Program for supporting me in this endeavor.

And thank you to my family, through whom I can do anything.

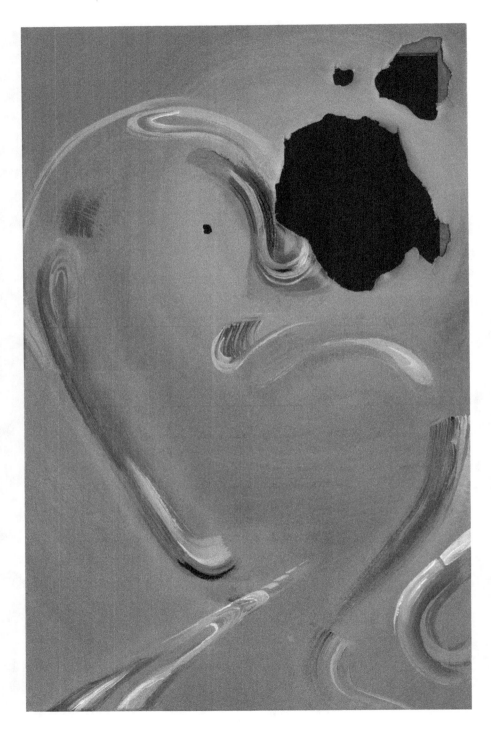

Artist Credit

Giulia Zappia is a twenty-year-old artist and designer from Rochester, New York. Beginning her education at the University of California Santa Barbara, Zappia is now transferring to the University of California Davis to complete her bachelor's in Design. Zappia combines physical media with digital aesthetics in her paintings to create emotional, abstract images. Her piece "Heartstrings" is featured in Maya Johnson's *Searching for a Black Writer* and focuses on love, turmoil, and ultimate acceptance.

"'Heartstrings' started with a letter. It began with prose and morphed into an image. It is about finding yourself amidst mourning your former life. I hope this piece has a unique message for everyone who views it. To me, its' center is love, but it is up to you to find meaning within it."

–Giulia Zappia

Artist Credit

Sonny Lata Yiu is a Chinese-Filipino painter, illustrator, and graphic designer. She grew up in the Bay Area with her loving and amazing parents, her best friend who also happens to be her twin sister, and her genius little brother. She has two gorgeous dogs, Duffy and Wybie, whom she spoils exceedingly.

She is currently attending UCSB's College of Creative Studies as a painting major and works on campus as a graphic designer. She loves to spend her free time reading, listening to Taylor Swift, and spending time with her family.

Printed in the USA
CPSIA information can be obtained
at www.ICGtesting.com
LVHW041919160624
783316LV00002B/174